Removing Unfreedoms

*"You have to show me how it relates to human life, how it relates
to their well-being and the freedom to be well. And the freedom not
only to be well, but the freedom to lead the kind of life they value
leading. That is the connection."*

Professor Amartya Sen, LSE 2003

Removing Unfreedoms

Citizens as Agents of Change in Urban Development

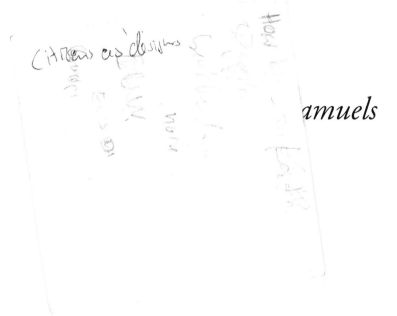

amuels

ITDG
PUBLISHING

Published by ITDG Publishing

The Schumacher Centre for Technology and Development, Bourton Hall, Bourton-on-Dunsmore, Rugby, Warwickshire, CV23 9QZ, UK

www.itdgpublishing.org.uk

First published 2005.

The editor acknowledges the following sources upon which she has drawn:

UN-Habitat Discussion Paper by Romi Khosla, Jane Samuels, Sikander Hasan and Budhi Mul, 2002

Freedom, Culture and Urban Revitalisation: The 21st Century Urban Scenario CD-ROM by Jane Samuels, 2002

Removing Unfreedoms DFID Report by Jane Samuels, 2003

Afghanistan Urban Recovery Proposal, The Aga Khan Trust for Culture

ISBN 1-85339-606-0

A catalogue record for this book is available from the British Library

ITDG Publishing is the publishing arm of the Intermediate Technology Development Group. Our mission is to build the skills and capacity of people in developing countries through the dissemination of information in all forms, enabling them to improve the quality of their lives and that of future generations.

Cover photograph of boys in central Georgia by Peter Nasmyth
Printed in the United Kingdom

Contents

Tables

Foreword b
Mrs Anna F

Under-Secret;
and Executive

I am pleased to see the publicatic
Citizens as Agents of Change in Urban
tion to the World Urban Forum in
rare opportunity to retool current u
by considering developmental freed(

Anwotyuda

tices already at the forefront of international policies. Central to this initiative is the drafting of a city-to-city urban framework formulated from the
work of the Nobel Laureate economist from India, Amartya Sen. The
Urban Freedom project was presented at the UN-World Habitat Day in
Brussels 2002 by the UN advisor and city planner Romi Khosla, working
with a team of consultants. The initiative is entitled 'Removing
Unfreedoms' as these are the vital concerns emphasized by Amartya Sen in
his work *Development as Freedom* (1999).

In our twenty-first century of globalization and free market forces, we
face an urban challenge unparalleled in our history. We have seen how
economic strategies have occupied the centre stage of narrower development theories, measuring more effective production of wealth and higher
terms of GNP growth or industrialization. There has been an underlying
assumption that the goals of economic-centred development are valid for
all human beings and that all human beings share common ideals and
principles. By contrast the Freedom Approach considers the issue of values
in a different way. Without assuming to distinguish specific human rights,
needs or goals, the Freedom Approach begins with the people and the
practical issue of understanding the varying moral and ethical issues that
govern the lives of different human beings across the world. If common
ideals and principles are shared, they will become evident by enabling the
capability of each and every individual citizen to be part of the process.
Development objectives would safeguard not pre-determine their choice to
lead the lives they value.

Removing Unfreedoms sets out to examine how developmental freedoms, attained through a variety of participatory processes and partnerships, provide development policy with new objectives. New evaluations and indicators are needed to monitor individual agencies and the social decision-making process within the community. The lessons learned regarding the success and obstructions of participation processes can be monitored by implementing Sen's five instruments of freedoms: political freedom, economic facilities, social opportunities, transparency guarantees and protective security. While current paradigms of sustainable development practice require specific targets, the Freedom Approach considers the individual citizens as the basic parameter, rather than a system, because in almost every case people, as agents of change, have come up with strategies to improve their livelihoods and overturn the barriers. Freedom becomes the means and end to a multi-objective development policy operational at the local, national and global level.

The intentions of the book share those outlined in the United Nations' Declaration on Cities, resolving to take effective measures to improve the conditions of human settlements. It is my belief that *developmental freedom* indicators will expand our information base and direct our approach to finding further ways to eliminate social deprivation at the grassroots level while challenging international obstacles to the lives of peoples living under colonial and foreign occupation.. The authors of the book make it clear that the management of this process will require a renewed political will and the mobilization and allocation of additional indicators and evaluations. Both strong and accountable public and international institutions are needed to provide an effective framework to measure the functioning of our cities across the developing/developed divide.

It is my hope the publication of this book will succeed to invite governments, the United Nations and other organizations across the globe to strengthen their commitment to sustainable human development by establishing these principles in new charters of urban governance. Their co-operation will further prioritize the role of inclusive social agency and participation through a city-to-city developmental freedom framework. By refocusing on the individual citizen as the agent of change this book contributes a valued source of inspiration and enrichment in developing UN-HABITAT's urban governance index and realizing the goals of our Global Governance Campaign internationally.

Mrs Anna Kajumulo Tibaijuka
September 2004

Preface

Cities are the places where new directions for development policies must emerge. They can either become settlements of intense poverty and community conflicts or centres of social, economic and political development. Cities can power both local and national development and this makes them the obvious sites to carry out the crucial changes in international policy advocated by the Nobel Laureate economist, Amartya Sen. In 1998 Sen's seminal work, *Development As Freedom*, was recognized by the Nobel committee for its contribution to economic development theory, establishing a fundamental new paradigm that defined new goals for international policy.

Sen evaluates societal arrangements in terms of their contribution to guaranteeing the substantive freedoms of individuals, who are viewed as active agents of change rather than as passive recipients of dispensed benefits. He specifies five freedoms as instruments to influence the potential and capabilities of the individual citizen. This participatory freedom-centred understanding of development strategies recognizes the positive role of free and sustainable individual agency: "Freedom is the primary end as well as the means to development" (Sen 1998).

This book argues that, in the light of Sen's work, there is an urgent need to modify international urban development policy frameworks and to modify the current range of evaluations and indicators that are used in order to inform policy makers. Such a goal would direct efforts to formulate an expanded policy framework. Additional evaluation methods would rely on democratic discussions with citizens to explore ways to enable people to lead the lives they value through the enjoyment of ever expanding freedoms.

Each of these freedoms would be evaluated in any city through a new set of indices that have yet to be formulated. Historically, designers and international agencies have been concerned with measuring various components of the city that contribute to its efficiency and services. Typically, UN-HABITAT resolutions have focused on the physical aspects of cities and have sponsored projects that were aimed at providing physical facilities to the needy in cities. With these new criteria there is a radical change in the focus of evaluating the functioning of cities. It is intended that this shift in focus will directly influence spontaneous municipal initiatives in cities through the emphasis on civic pressures and expectancies.

The urban policy proposal described in this book was researched and developed over the past three years by Romi Khosla and myself in collaboration with Amartya Sen, Michael Mutter at the UK's Department for International Development (DFID), Sikander Hasan and Budhi Mulyawan. The concept was originally proposed by Romi, who for 25 years was the principal director of a planning and architectural practice in Delhi. He trained as an economist with Amartya Sen at Cambridge and then at the Architectural Association in London. During the past six years, as a principal international consultant to the UNDP, UNESCO, UNOPS and WTO, he has spent considerable time initiating development projects linked to urban renewal in Central Asia, Tibet, Egypt, Bulgaria, Romania, Cyprus, and Palestine.

More recently, Romi returned to the work of Amartya Sen in order to appreciate how the solutions to urban conflicts and poverty could be addressed through applying Sen's economic considerations. He first began to explore his proposal with a developer in Istanbul. In March 2001, discussions opened with Michael Mutter – then DFID Senior Architecture and Urban Development Adviser – and myself, a colleague from some years back. Michael was in a unique position as an urban development adviser to the UK government who had built up a perspective on development from both supporting new multi-lateral approaches at one level and, at the same time, providing direct support to entirely local initiatives. Our discussions explored an emerging formulation process for cities and urban master plans, an application of Sen's ideas as a coherent policy approach to international development cooperation.

In May 2002, Mutter encouraged Michael Parkes, then director of the UN-HABITAT Liaison Office in Brussels, to commission our research and a discussion paper to be launched at the UN-World Habitat Day in October 2002 at the Palais d'Egmont, in the presence of HRH Prince Fellippe and Mrs Tibajuika, Under-Secretary-General and Executive Director of UN-HABITAT. Michael Mutter then directed us to material that provided a rare opportunity to reconsider a variety of current development approaches, practices and evaluations with the aim of creating a shared freedom policy framework.

The draft discussion paper was shown to Amartya Sen, then Master of Trinity College Cambridge, to obtain his response. In further preparation for the UN-World Habitat Day launch, we later returned to Trinity College Cambridge to film an interview between Romi and Amartya Sen to reassess key questions Romi had pulled forth from the research. This interview later became edited into a film by Janet Boston at TVE, *Agents of Change*, which was broadcast on BBC World television and produced as a CD-ROM by the Development Planning Unit at University College, London. Copies were given out to all the participants at the UN-World Habitat Day.

The enthusiastic endorsement by Amartya Sen and so many participating development representatives encouraged Michael to approve further DFID research which began in April 2003. On this occasion he identified the local initiatives of three NGOs, that of Homeless International based in the UK, the National Slum Dwellers Federations and SPARC based in Mumbai, India. This time we were to explore whether these ideas made any sense to the homeless, the pavement and slum dwellers on the ground. More depth to the ideas emerged and these were debated by an emerging group of practitioners – from international agencies, activists, academics and the slum dwellers themselves – when we finally brought them all together for a colloquium at the London School of Economics attended by Professor Amartya Sen and Lord Meghnad Desai.

Removing Unfreedoms: Citizens as Agents of Change in Urban Development is an analysis and record of all these events, including further dialogues in which one or the other of us have further presented the inspiration of these policies to those in India, Vienna, Australia, Geneva, Turkey, Afghanistan and Iraq. As Michael believes, "it is a presentation of an evolving project, a discourse of real events, bringing together the life experiences of human beings as agents of change to the table of the policy makers".

Early this year it was my good fortune to meet Nesreen Berwari, with whom Michael had been working in Iraq. Nesreen is currently Iraq's Minister for municipalities and public works, leader of the localized development practice and a recent recipient of a UN-HABITAT prize for her work on the welfare of the displaced and vulnerable persons in Iraqi Kurdistan – which assisted more than 4000 destroyed communities and towns. Her introduction to this book, written with Michael, underlines her widening concern both for the role of women, for which she has been a leading voice in her country, and for the Kurdish people and the ethnic minorities. In a new Iraq the minorities can be equal partners in cooperation through the adoption of these proposed development policies. In her opinion, the operation of a Freedom Approach, with an emphasis on localized development decision making, provides an enviable model for any emerging democratic country with new institutions for coordinated municipal initiatives.

Finally, when taking into account the cumulative experiences, support and contributions of all these remarkable people, I am reminded of the day when first receiving Romi's proposal, 'The Untitled City', as he then called this work. His opening words were a reflection on his own lifetime objectives:

> *"It is very important for me to speculate and evolve ideas about the problems that are going to come and whether it is Tibet, Kosova, Palestine, Cyprus, Afghanistan, or this cities project, it always remains important to me to be optimistic in my predictions."*

We trust this book provides the reader with an optimistic and timely application of Sen's ideals to urban development policy. In the words of Michael Mutter: "Here is an effective and satisfying way of engaging in this process – of promoting local initiatives in a way that can be recognized and respected on the world stage". The book does not claim to be a comprehensive review. As yet there exist no complete case studies that have applied a Freedom Approach to project design and participation processes with monitoring and evaluation assessments. However, this does not undervalue the significance of this book, rather we hope it provides the opportunity to re-evaluate the existing urban environment and development policy and consider the value of indices that measure degrees of freedom of social agency rather than relying exclusively on measuring degrees of poverty. Good governance therefore becomes not an end, but the means of delivering greater freedom to the inhabitants of the city.

Jane Samuels
September 2004

Acknowledgements

A great many people have contributed to the events and dialogues documented in this book. We would like to thank Michael Parkes, Senior Adviser in Architecture and Urban Development at DFID, who first agreed to commission the UN-HABITAT discussion paper presented at the World Habitat Day in Brussels. Mrs Anna Tibaijuka, Under-Secretary-General and Executive Director at UN-HABITAT for both her original enthusiasm and contributing the foreword to this book.

We also thank Michael Mutter, past Senior Architectural and Urban Planning Adviser in the Infrastructure and Urban Development Department at DFID, who believes in the work and most importantly the people. His determination and extensive experience were responsible for enabling the funding, directing the research to include everyone, and for the overall success of the Removing Unfreedoms project. His colleague Dr Yusuf Samiullah, from DFID South Africa, presided over the lively interchanges at the LSE Colloquium and interpreted these thoughts for the development community.

We are honoured and extremely grateful to Professor Amartya Sen for his inspiring support, film interviews, invaluable guidance and discussions when attending the LSE Colloquium on 7 July 2003. Equally, we are indebted to his colleague and friend Lord Meghnad Desai for his dynamic contribution that day. Antonio Vigilante, Co-ordinator from the UNDP office in Cairo, who travelled to London to be with us, for his presentation to the Colloquium and contribution to the book. He has provided long-standing and continued support for this project. We must also acknowledge the help of Professor Pat Wakely, for his continuous assistance at the Development Planning Unit, University College London, and Professor Nabeel Hamdi, for offering CENDEP as a base to do the research, for his numerous consultations and reviews, and for chairing the presentations at LSE.

Thanks also go to many others. Jo Beall who hosted the LSE Colloquium and the Development Studies Institute (DESTIN) at the London School of Economics. Rick Davies for his experience and innovative work on monitoring and evaluations that aided our research. Ruth McLeod from Homeless International. Sheela Patel and all those at SPARC, including Sundar Burra, Celine D'cruz and the Mahila Milan Women's Savings Group, the National Slum Dwellers Federation of India and Jockin, Arpurthan, their remarkable President (who is also President of the Slum Dwellers International) for bringing us in to the heart of their city, Mumbai. B.K. Agarwal, past secretary of housing for the Government of Maharashtra, India for taking part in the Mumbai workshop.

Nick Hall and Smita Biswas at WSP as the key coordinators and participants of the Mumbai workshop and LSE Colloquium. Tamlyn Samuels who filmed the LSE Colloquium and secured all the documentation. David Satterthwaite for his solid consultation and meeting at IIED. Alison Barret of Cities Alliance for joining us in Mumbai and Jolly Shah from CENDEP for hours and hours of transcriptions. Jeremy Holland who provided the participatory rights assessment methodologies. There were those who journeyed from Africa, Columbia and India. In particular we would like to thank Alberto Lopes from Rio de Janeiro for his valuable contribution on the favelas, which is included in this book. Sikander Hasan who contributed extensively to the original UN-HABITAT paper and Budhi Mulyawan.

Finally, Toby Milner, Ginny Gilmore and all those at ITDG Publishing for their expertise and support to make this book possible under remarkable circumstances. Charlie Wright, who held the objective of what was at hand editing, kind guidance and friendship. Nick Wates for his publishing experience. David Cadmon and Ed Posey most valued senior advisors. Peter Nasmyth for the cover photograph.

The CD-ROM, *21st Century Urban Scenario*, produced by Anna Soave and Sikander Hasan, includes the original UN-HABITAT discussion paper, the TVE film *Agents of Change* and the filmed interview with Romi Khosla and Amartya Sen. It is available from the Development Planning Unit, University College London (see http://www.ucl.ac.uk/dpu – under publications.

The publication of this book is funded by the UK's Department for International Development. The views expressed in the publications are those of the individual authors and do not necessarily reflect the views of DFID.

All the events, dialogues, transcripts and research referred to in this book have been documented on our website www.removingunfreedoms.org.

Introduction

Nesreen Berwari and Michael Mutter

Over the period of more than half a century since World War II we have seen nations assisting nations with tremendous resources, both financial and human, flowing from those with more to those with less. While progress has indeed been made, we remain daunted by the prevalence and persistence of poverty in all too much of our everyday lives, in all too much of a world that has seen transport and communication technology bringing us closer together. Regardless of our own personal wealth, advances in information and telecommunication technology mean that it is all but impossible to remain unaware of the poverty that exists in our larger world.

During the past five decades or so the vehicle used by industrialized Western nations in assisting lesser-developed countries to alleviate poverty has been driven by economics and economic growth, together with the quantitative methods applied to measure its status and progress, or lack thereof. It has been generally assumed that as economic indicators increase, poverty levels decrease, living standards rise and the quality of life improves. Much of the impetus for this approach is the expediency of nation-to-nation assistance largely based on the requirements of nationally oriented bilateral and multilateral development programmes. With the advantage of decades of hindsight, history, experience and observation, however, we see too often that the results that were sought remain elusive.

The dimensions of development and poverty alleviation obviously include more than economics and economic growth. There are political and social issues that may often contain root factors that either cause poverty and/or inhibit progress to prosperity and a personal sense of well-being. During the past fifty years, the concepts of development and poverty reduction themselves have been developing and moving from being nationally-focused to being more people-focused.

What is really happening at the ordinary person level? What is the effect of international and national development policies and programmes at the level at which people feel directly? What is the public interest and how is it best addressed both at the personal and at the national levels? Do rising economic indicators credibly portray an improved quality of life, satisfying to a country's citizens? Answering these questions has moved the process more towards 'sustainable, community-based, people-participatory policies and programmes', often largely determined and designed in contexts far removed from 'target beneficiaries' and 'impact areas'.

At a more fundamental level, moral imperatives do not allow us the luxury of a fully rewarding and satisfying life in a world where so many of our fellow human beings suffer in indignity and injustice. More recently, to offer another measure of human development, national development and poverty alleviation are increasingly addressed through the Human Development Index (HDI) that combines life expectancy, literacy and per capita income – adjusted for real purchasing power. HDI methods may also include the evaluation of environment and freedom factors, gender and regional differences, income distribution, etc.

A more unique approach is that of the Kingdom of Bhutan's Gross National Happiness (GNH) philosophy that guides national policy making. This more people-centred approach focuses on factors that undermine human dignity and the value of human life. It involves the process of promoting development and ensuring freedom from the uncertainty of survival and want of basic needs.

The aim of development is largely to address the effects of poverty that undermine human dignity. While few countries are prepared or willing to adapt and apply Bhutan's innovative GNH philosophy, there is indeed progress beyond the rather dry quantitative economics and economic growth approach, and the slightly less impersonal HDI version. An exciting alternative focuses on processes that allow 'freedoms' to break out in a manner that allows people to live as they choose. This rightly shifts the focus from those who aim to intervene in 'right ways', to those with the most fundamental interest in development interventions, the people themselves.

The alternative more than shifts the focus. The 'target beneficiaries' become the interventionists by intervening into their own lives in an environment that enables them to live the life they choose. The enabling environment offers expanding opportunities for freedoms. It goes beyond time-worn efforts that often reduce poverty without coming closer to exploiting these freedom opportunities.

Nobel Laureate Amartya Sen has coined the term 'unfreedoms' to help us understand why poverty is currently so pervasive in modern society, and why this need not be the case. The concept of 'Removing Unfreedoms' describes how less advantaged people can nevertheless enjoy the same kinds of freedoms that prevail in so-called developed countries. It requires policies that remove obstacles to allow less advantaged people to apply their energies in ways that obviate the need for specific aid interventions. These policies are generated locally, devised by the people themselves, and championed at the

national level in a manner that is supported by international policies that attract support where, if and when it is needed. This evolution contains the ingredients of a major paradigm shift with the power to accelerate substantial development and poverty alleviation.

So what does Removing Unfreedoms mean to ordinary people and what are the implications for policy makers? How can political initiatives respond to the concept of Removing Unfreedoms? This Introduction compares successes in global policy making with successes in national and local policy making. Both are part of the intricate web of politics that ultimately enables development by the people themselves, for themselves.

What is really happening at the ordinary person level? Slums along the Jakarta to Tanjung Priok railway, Indonesia.

(Jan Banning/ Panos)

The Habitat Agenda

The UN's focal point for human settlements is UN-HABITAT. Formerly the United Nations Centre for Human Settlements, since December 2001 the Centre has been upgraded to a full UN Programme for Human Settlements and has been mandated with the task of leading the world in policies for urban development, regeneration and processes that can improve the lives of slum dwellers.[1] The international community – led by DFID on behalf of the UK – has helped UN-HABITAT re-establish itself as both a global policy body as well as the leading global agency for coordinating international implementation strategies.

In June 1996, as part of the decade of global UN conferences, UN-HABITAT convened the second World Habitat Conference in Istanbul – the first having been in Vancouver in 1976. At this conference the world's national governments, in conjunction with the global representatives of local authorities and NGOs, agreed the Habitat Agenda – essentially agreeing to recognize and help the poorest within the context of the development of the growing villages and cities of the world. In many ways, the Habitat Agenda has thus laid an internationally agreed framework for new and further approaches to poverty reduction, such as the concepts represented by Removing Unfreedoms.

How has global policy for the development of human settlements evolved since the international agreement on the Habitat Agenda? There was so much hope and enthusiasm created at Istanbul, and in many ways this has informed the global debate on the development of human settlements to become more inclusive and to recognize the respect for the contribution to the economy made by the poorest – commonly occupying the SLUMS of the rapidly growing villages, towns, cities and mega-cities of the developing countries of the world. UN-HABITAT's two global campaigns – on striving towards better urban governance and allowing slum dwellers to have security of tenure in their homes – also reflect the kind of thinking that Professor Sen is putting forward.

A short word on SLUMS

Proud slum dwellers, members of the million strong and growing international movement Slum (or Shack) Dwellers International (SDI), provided the key presentation at the UN Headquarters in New York in June 2001 for Istanbul+5, the review of progress made on the implementation of the Habitat Agenda in the five years since it was agreed in Istanbul. They built their full sized 'model' house and community toilet block on the marble floor of the foyer where it would attract maximum attention, including that of the Secretary General.

The term 'slums', however, is a term not used in many parts of the world, hence the inclusion of the term 'shacks'. It is not used, for example, in Arab and middle-eastern countries where there is a greater understanding of the contribution of the poorest within the community. In Asia, the term is clear. In Africa, the term 'shack' is more often used, although the growing SLUMS of great and important cities, such as Nairobi, Kenya, are themselves extraordinary places where the contribution of the poor to society in general is steadily becoming recognized. Whatever the circumstances of origin or existence, SDI – together with the UK based global NGO Homeless International – have a coordination role in portraying the plight of slum-dwellers wherever they may be, but primarily a positive role in portraying what it is that they can do for themselves, given the legitimate and legalized opportunity.

Localizing development opportunity

What, therefore, has been the response of the international community – the International Development Cooperation Agencies (ICDAs), those, for example, representing the Organisation of Economic Cooperation and Development (OECD) governments in considering a localized development approach? [2] Emerging from the post-war Marshall Plan, the Paris-based OECD has become the watchdog of official development assistance, the measure of aid that the developed countries give for international development. The OECD has itself commissioned its Environment Committee to look into the implications for the environment of the current massive expansion of urban areas. Their website demonstrates an acute awareness of the issues, having set up and pursued a sub-committee on People and Urban Environment Issues – see www.oecd.org/dac/urbenv.

As observed above, the Nairobi based UN-HABITAT is the primary repository of information on the development of human settlements, as existing and in the future. They measure this responsibility through the Global Urban Observatory drawing information from national and local urban observatories, such as the one that the University of Westminster works on in the UK. Others have been set up with equivalent socio-economic and physical development responsibilities worldwide. UN-HABITAT provides the global coordination.

The World Bank has returned to its urban portfolio of projects, recognizing that providing support to poor people in urban areas is a key to reducing poverty generally. Urban areas grow out of expanding villages and people are drawn to urban locations in search of better opportunities, especially for their children. Improvements in living conditions in urban areas not only satisfy this urge to join the modern world – so difficult in oppressive rural locations – but also to provide the services that can help people lead better lives and thereby become more productive elements within their societies. Everyone wins, including rural-based people who have the opportunity to respond to the increased demand for rural production to feed the productive city. What is important is the development of governance arrangements that ensure that the process is equitably shared. Removing Unfreedoms is a way of ensuring this fairness.

As a response UN-HABITAT and the World Bank have together initiated the Cities Alliance. This aims to bring a further degree of reality to the implementation capacity of cities and local governments by practically investing in infrastructure and improved environment that will reduce poverty by enabling far more people to benefit from the opportunities afforded by inclusive urban development.

The key to local development policy making is the involvement of the political representation of the people and communities at the local level – primarily through local government, municipal and service authorities, however they may be constituted. The collective associations of local government at national and international levels provide a stable capacity for municipal level knowledge of development practice. The Cities Alliance has successfully built a platform whereby the municipalities facilitate their urban communities in taking a policy lead in local development strategies for slum upgrading.

Amongst the instruments that the Cities Alliance has promoted is the Community-led Infrastructure Finance Facility – CLIFF.[3] This is an important international concept. CLIFF has been born out of a significant piece of research into ways in which the urban poor have access to development finance.[4] CLIFF seeks to bring initial finance to established community groups so that they can develop their plans and demonstrate their capacity to lead a local development process in conjunction with their local governments and the local private sector finance institutions.

CLIFF built on earlier work developed as the City-Community Challenge Fund (C3), launched in 1999 by Clare Short, then Secretary of State for International Development, at a peer-level meeting of slum dwellers from the entire SDI network, meeting in London.[5] C3 brings additional donor funding to augment small-scale proposals developed by the communities themselves, again in conjunction with their local governments.

Homeless International has promoted the 'Inclusive City' website. This brings together the various actions at a grassroots level of communities developing their own policies and putting them into action. The collective initiatives provide a groundswell of opinion and demonstration of development effectiveness that governments at local, municipal and national policy-making levels have come to respect. The critical mass of the community, when organized around a collective approach, builds an assurance of strength that then provides a realistic platform for challenging the idea that government is responsible for the provision of all the services required for inclusive urban development.

Experience has shown that effective joint responsibility is drawn from the concept of savings. In each of the SDI groups the central theme of daily saving schemes is paramount. Daily saving schemes provide the backbone of the community approach to Removing Unfreedoms. In Mumbai, India, Sheela Patel – head of the Society for Area Resource Centres, SPARC – has pioneered the acceptance of the informal group Mahila Milan ('women working together') as a positive force for change.

She has formed a strategic alliance with the indefatigable chairman of the Indian National Slum Dwellers' Federation. This is a prime example of people exercising the Removing Unfreedoms approach in reality.

Developing the processes where the community leads the development process to bring services that meet these objectives has been central to the work undertaken by Nesreen Berwari with communities in Iraqi Kurdistan. Displaced citizens re-learnt their role in becoming responsible for designing their reconstruction efforts, through their choice to return to their destroyed communities, to rebuild their homes and to make improvements that did not exist before – such as motor vehicle accessible roads, piped water systems, schools, primary health centres and civic facilities. Earlier unfreedoms were removed and the people responded by voluntarily choosing to return to live in difficult rural environments they had not experienced in decades. It was their land, their home and their life. It was their choice. More than 50,000 families made that choice. This 'freedom to development' approach, with the emphasis on localized development decision making, provides an enviable model of coordinated municipal development for the whole of the newly emerging democratic Iraq and its institutions.

An interesting point to note is the way in which men and women relate to each other in these processes. More central control is exerted by women than they are generally given credit for. A Kurdish woman is not affectionately referred to as the Minister of the Interior for no reason. They are the guardians of finance. They bring together the various levels of work that are often carried out by men. Although policy makers may more often be men than women, the central role that women play in the development process is respected. In Iraqi Kurdistan, the role of women was also strengthened, for example, by their being trained in maintaining village water systems, and by the acceptance of them in that role. The often traumatic history of the region left numerous widow-headed households. These women assumed non-traditional decision-making responsibilities that have strengthened their roles in society.

Global policy framework for human settlements

Localizing the Habitat Agenda is the challenge that policy makers need to address so that ordinary people can be recognized for the contribution that they already make to the development process.[6] By using the Removing Unfreedoms approach, the task is made that much more comprehensible to the policy makers themselves. This is how it would work locally. What is important is the ways in which progress is measured.

By using Sen's five measures of freedom as development as a way of describing the governance performance of cities, municipalities and their regions and, indeed, their urbanizing villages, we arrive at some common

A Kurdish refugee
returns from
Turkey to find her
house in ruins.

(Frits Meyst/
Panos)

language and understanding for measuring progress that means something to people locally. For example we could begin to ascertain ways in which:

- for political freedom we would measure the degree of participation as perceived by the people locally

- for economic facilities we would measure the effectiveness of production and exchange as locally as possible

- for social opportunities we would consider the degree of equity in the make up of the fabric of society and the degree to which it is changing

- for transparency and guarantees we would use a local system of accountability

- for protective security we would use a simple security assessment process as determined by people locally.

This development of the Habitat Agenda framework provides a system for people to devise their own parameters, methods of participation and measures, locally, and yet it also provides a way in which both national governments and international supporters can participate and offer a legitimate means of intervention that can be welcomed, respected and made useful for ordinary people. There are so many prospects for the future. For example, UN-HABITAT is assisting the new sovereign government of Iraq in building policies that enable people to develop their own community strategies for a new future. In this way, Iraq will take part in, and contribute to, this new global approach to localized development along the lines envisaged in the Habitat Agenda.

Amartya Sen's freedom-centered approach places the beneficiary in the driver's seat. The driver is not only the driver; he or she owns the car/bus/truck, and the captain owns the ship. Those in a position to provide assistance may be sought to ride along to offer guidance and support by reading and interpreting available roadmaps and adding resource support. But the choice to proceed straight, or to turn left or right, belongs exclusively to the driver and captain. An enabling environment that offers expanding opportunities of choice of freedoms' roads is a powerful construct. It is this empowerment of individuals that is more likely to lead to real development that is heartfelt and satisfying, that goes far beyond poverty alleviation being little more than a matter of poverty reduction.

Part I

Development
and Urbanization

- 1 -

Cities, Conflict and Visions

Our concern to improve the conditions of contemporary cities is by its nature a compassionate quest. How does one think about being compassionate? How can one enable citizens living in communities to expand their lives with measures that they value? There is a distinction here between a search for ways to improve the lives of citizens, and the search for ways that enable citizens to live the life that they value and that remove the obstructions that look down on and coerce people to live a life that others value. These obstructions we shall call 'unfreedoms', a term coined by Amartya Sen. They can be imposed by others from within or from outside a community in order to prevent the expression of such freedom of choice.

This book explores why and how we must go about implementing new policies which would enable citizens to live a life of freely chosen personalized values, values that one can choose to change from time to time. We believe the realization of this potential is what lies at the root of what individuals, communities, regions and nations aspire to. Nonetheless we seem to be passing through a period of history, once again, when dominant ideologies have taken over the agenda of the future and there is a growing righteousness, a sort of arrogance that refuses to accept or absorb diverging interests and a multiplicity of interpretations.

When we view the events of the past century, as well as recent events that have already made headlines, there appears a growing tendency to obstruct people, communities and indeed whole nations from living according to their own beliefs and values. We have lived through the most violent and destructive century in human history; the collective memories of at least two generations have been gutted in the trenches, prisons and urban rubble of two world wars, two civil wars, two violent revolutions, and this century has already begun with a high score in Africa, Yugoslavia, Afghanistan, Iraq and who knows where next, perhaps Iran. In the order of world affairs there seems a growing universalization of pre-selected humanist values, a sort of abrogation by the powerful nations to universalize values that they think are valuable.

War widows
wearing burqas
wait for food
parcels at a Red
Cross aid
distribution
centre, shortly
after the Taliban
takeover of
Kabul,
Afghanistan.

(Martin Adler/
Panos)

These are very narrowly interpreted and give the right to impose and coerce weaker communities and nations. Thus 'human rights, 'democratic freedom', 'civil liberties', 'war crimes', 'the war on terrorism', the World Trade Organization and the like have become part of a doctrine whose righteousness supersedes national histories and cultures.

We are entering the twenty-first century with a world order in which the strong nations want the weaker nations to live by enforced doctrines. These are nothing more than the impositions of unfreedoms – the consequences of the transformations of the old imperial attitudes about the superiority or inferiority of civilizations. But these impositions exist not only at the gross national levels. The impact is felt much deeper down by citizens as international finance has become a sort of vulture that hovers over nations and communities, picking on what meets its fancy and then flying on, while generally avoiding productive investment in fixed geographical locations. The long-term effects of these global economies reach into the future, increasing poverty levels enormously. [1]

Take, for example, the experience of those working over recent years in emergency programmes for the urban poor in Bulgaria, Kosovo, Romania and Palestine where poverty levels have reduced urban life to a sort of bondage. Some countries such as Serbia, Kosovo, Afghanistan and Iraq are in deep crisis. There are others such as Pakistan who are on the edge of crisis, and then there are countries like India who have been driven to the edge of crisis by mass poverty bequeathed by colonialism. This is: "poverty in the modern sense, involving insecurity, which is qualitatively different from what existed earlier" (Patnaik 2002).

At the risk of generalizing, it could be said that there are certain common features to countries in crises:

- The literature and analysis of the ideological systems of the twentieth century seems to have become irrelevant.

- There is a desperate search for immediate and effective results and connected to this is a growing disillusionment with existing national government.

- There is a search for new systems of government.

- The idea of a centralized authoritarian government needs to be replaced by a government of participation and shared management.

- There is a need to harness the help of the private sector, NGOs and civil society to find particular solutions to problems.

- National or state level solutions to problems must be increasingly realigned in favour of tailor-made community-based solutions. Indeed, each community and each individual has special problems and generic solutions will no longer be seen as useful.

At present these characteristics are not universally agreed. The increasing levels of urban unfreedoms brought about through the impositions of strong nations and the force of global finance and Third World debt currently arrest any possible solutions for many nations in crisis and their citizens.

However, we do not want pass a solely negative judgement on recent history. We can look to the example of India, an ancient civilization that gained its independence from 200 years of colonial rule by non-violence. That fact alone fills all of us with hope for the future. For while it seems at one end that coercions and unfreedoms seem to be growing, it is also true that enormous liberties have also been gained through the modernization processes of the last two centuries. The process of modernization which began sometime in the nineteenth century was, and still remains to-day, a part of an earlier more basic search for greater human freedom. If we were to disregard, for the moment, the values of freedom in the realm of ancient philosophy and epics, and refer only to more recent historic events, one could say that the first momentous event that transformed the potential to be free was initiated by the French Revolution at the end of the eighteenth century. The principle theorist of the revolution, the Marquis de

The Marquis de
Condorcet.

Condorcet, was also the main founder of the discipline of social choice theory, the subject central to Sen's Freedom Approach which advocates participation in the field of developmental economics (Dreze and Sen 2002). The value of participation was further taken forward by the socialist revolution in Russia in October 1917 that transformed the Russian Revolution from liberal-democratic to socialist in character.

Despite the recent collapse of socialism, we must not be misled into believing, as Prabhat Patnaik explains,

"that the freedom project unleashed initially by the French Revolution, of which the socialist project constituted a legacy, has also collapsed. Indeed, the collapse of the extant socialist project itself was predicted on the promise of greater freedom, but there were severe constraints imposed by existing material conditions which always limit the range of possibilities and prevent the spontaneous outcome of people's activities from coinciding with their intentions."

Patnaik, 2002

The project for gaining greater freedom remains very much valid and alive. Therefore the issue before us is this: if the socialist project has collapsed and has been replaced by religious and ethnic fundamentalism, how do we continue to search for human freedom? Fundamentalism and racism is about imposing unfreedoms on people. Socialism was meant to provide a buffer against such impositions which it failed to do, indeed it increased certain unfreedoms for citizens.

Inevitably the boundaries of human freedom are difficult to define. Each historical era, each individual, community or country defines its freedom in different ways at different times. Freedom could be seen as a relative concept without absolutes, and yet boundaries to human freedom exist and it is possible to define the content of this freedom. A long and well-established link exists between the pronouncements of thinkers, writers and philosophers who have advocated and described freedom and our present perceptions about human rights, democracy and free movement of trade.

These perceptions have been substantially built on a body of literature and awareness of the nature of freedom. More recently, Amartya Sen has explored further some of these wider aspects of freedom in his seminal work *Development As Freedom* (Sen 1999), where he has linked freedom to development and hence re-described this almost abstract notion to the physical condition of society. This work has significant implications for our perception of cities as instruments of development, as increasingly Sen's ideas have relevance to global governance programmes.

When considering the urban reconstruction efforts in the Balkans and Palestine much of what was seen and experienced there by those implementing regeneration projects becomes comprehensible after referring to Sen's work. For in all these hidden and expressed conflicts and conditions of suffering, where some form of crisis or bondage had destroyed the futures of citizens, the problem was not poverty per se. It was the imposition of unfreedoms by the strong on the weak and the complete absence of compassion. Poverty was the manifestation of these imposed unfreedoms. A people become poor or get impoverished because they are prevented from initiating change. The poor, the minorities, the inhabitants of middle cities are often treated like patients and treatments are prescribed to them. If, on the other hand, we regard every citizen as an agent of change, a person with a unique potential and capability, new dynamic solutions would constantly appear.

There is a need, therefore, to expand the range of solutions to the problem of human poverty and human suffering and to search afresh for ways to achieve a situation where continuous improvements to the goals of human development can become policy for our urban settlements.

Urbanization

In order to describe new urban polices we will briefly review the history of urban development and the origins of our contemporary city formations. The word 'urbanization' was coined by a Spaniard, Ildefonso Cerda, in 1867 to define what he thought was a new phenomenon and child of the Industrial Revolution (Choay 1969). The city as we perceive it today is a product of nineteenth century ideas. During the late eighteenth and early nineteenth centuries, empirical and clinical research and the so-called discoveries began to transform the systems of knowledge in Europe. During this time irrefutable principles and laws began to be applied to all aspects of human affairs, and the city too came under this anvil. Like the anatomical

inquiries on the human body, the telescopic discoveries of the universe, and the skull measuring exercises on African tribes, the city became an object of inquiry and measurement. New ideas about the city began to be propagated with the support of this new epistemology – uniformities and common aspects were emphasised, common patterns detected and universal solutions advocated for the enhancement of civilization. This was part of the enlightenment trend, a socio-political trend that tried to correct the shortcomings of existing cities.

The new ideal city was to contain a new socio-political order with new morals, new relationships between the workers and factory owners, new manners and new modes of life lived according to the new values of the liberated bourgeoisie. The industrial city that was forced to house the migration from the country to supply the workforce for the new factories became regarded as a diseased body, diseased spiritually and morally, that needed to be cured. Two schools of thought emerged. One advocated surgical regularization while another advocated burying the diseased city and resurrecting it in the form of ideal paradises set in the countryside. Progress was viewed as a sequence of specific regulatory town laws that were linked to a higher level of regional laws, which in turn were part of an imagined harmonious logical system that could fulfil human needs, with good behaviour and high morals at its core. These early ideas about cities were to a large extent platonic in that all the problems of the post-industrial revolution cities cited simple mono-solutions.

Prior to these 'enlightened' ideas about cities, urban settlements had been perceived as almost symbiotic systems that existed in history synchronically and in a slowly transforming status quo. The living together of dissimilar organisms in which mutual associations are beneficial goes contrary to the idealization of cities. The nineteenth century city visionaries regarded such a view of the static city as part of the spiritual and intellectual confusion of the classical age of superstition. Clerical rules of

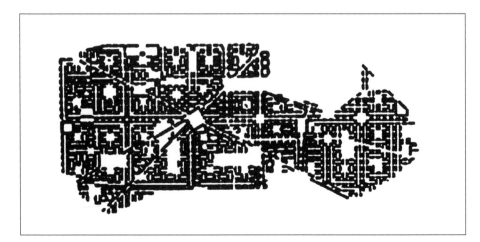

Plan of Barcelona
by Cerda

conduct needed to be replaced by civic rules and regulations about city administration.

The notion of idealizing the city as an object that would contain the moral order of the future took two quite separate routes. One route sought to enshrine the new enlightened moral order in regularization, rules and regulations, while the other took to inventing a new urban order, set in the countryside, equidistant between the dangers of urban slums and the village, a sort of new paradise for the inhabitants of the new moral order. We need to look at both of these in turn because both these ideals have continued to influence our current perceptions about cities to date. The idealization of the city transformed by development and strict rules and regulations has governed much of post-war European city formation.

The other ideal – a paradise city proposal, has, on the other hand, influenced early experiments with garden cities in England and Germany and, on a much larger scale, recent city formation in other parts of the world such as Canberra, Brasilia, Chandigarh, and Islamabad. In both these idealizations, the need for the city to be stylistically uniform and compatible with a single ideal was a pre-conditional assumption. It was also inevitable that the formation of such an ideal meant that restrictions had to be imposed on any other solutions that did not conform to that ideal. These restrictions were the unfreedoms of the time and they have continued to remain as the coercive regulatory powers of city administrations in most cities of the world. Far from being acknowledged and reformed, the restrictions have increased and are replicated globally as a monoculture city model. For example in physical formations, these restrictions are related to the type of housing that is acceptable and to the use of open spaces for social uses. For instance, the carnival uses the linear space of streets and obstructs traffic. Fetes are more acceptable as they can be contained in plazas. The restrictions enforced to maintain a stylistically uniform city are coercive because such regulations tend to obliterate the multiple distinctions and visions that the wide range of migrants value as part of their own identities.

Paris: the idealized city

In European history there is one city that has become a model for subsequent administrations around the world. Consider the transformation of Paris by Baron Haussmann who became head of the Prefecture of Paris in 1853. He, together with Napoleon III, began a surgical process on Paris that was to idealize the city and finally tame the restless lives of the urban peasant migrants.

The enormous human influx into the European city caused by the opportunities of industrialization, as well as push factors in the countryside, trans-

Baron Haussmann

formed the medieval city into an overcrowded metropolis. The symbiotic social systems that characterized pre-industrial cities broke down and the authorities began to lose control of the city. They reacted by viewing the city as a law and order problem. It was a problem that had been created, not so much by crime, but by the co-habitation of the differing realities and values that peasants and small farmers brought with them to the town. The migrants wanted to live an urban life that they valued and the authorities had to coerce them to live the life that the authorities valued.

The planners reacted severely and planned the regularization of the city after they had quantified the problem. Haussmann's transformation of Paris became a model for many cities in Europe (Barcelona, Antwerp, Dresden and London) and continues to be the model for city transformation in the developing world. Some 60 per cent of the buildings and streets of present day Paris were built in Haussmann's time. This was what we could call the gentrification of Paris as it restricted the values and alternative lifestyles of a largely immigrant population.

In looking at the transformations, there are good, bad and ugly effects. The large-scale sewers, the safe drinking water supply and the street lighting network changed Paris into a better, healthier place to live for all its inhabitants. Haussmann's surgery affected Paris' streets, buildings, parks and services in the crowded city. Prior to his time, Paris had experienced rather gentler additions and alterations to its accommodations and spaces. But Napoleon III had a different vision that needed to idealize the social lifestyle and values of the city. Paris was to be made into a model for prosperity and propriety. He needed to restructure and cut through the old fabric and thus create openings, vistas and grand avenues – these new imperial artefacts could only be created if the middle city of classical times was cut through.

The new streets that were laid down were to become the containers and barriers to the organic lifestyles of the migrants. These streets were to encompass a new style of living that revolved around salons, street cafés, stores and restaurants. They were to provide the direct routes to the railway station, the parks, hospitals, business districts, government buildings and the gendarmerie. Neither Baron Haussmann nor Napoleon was concerned with the multiple social, political or cultural diversities of inhabitants other than the gentry. The Paris transformation was a large scale monolithic solution of an ideal which gave no space for alternatives. Small scale complexities and interconnections were substituted by a monumental simplicity. They were inevitably resisted – for example, the resistance by the middle city inhabitants at the Rue Antoine in 1848 and the demolition of Boulevard Saint Michel in 1856. Place de la Concorde is the imperial macro-city ideal, appropriating the spaces of the middle city and boxing them off behind high facades.

Of course, our question is not whether this could have been done another way at that time. Rather it is seeing what happened in Paris and other European cities in the nineteenth century and asking if there is today another way to enable the alternative lifestyles of different immigrants to flourish in a city without coercing them to conform to some assumed higher value system? It is this city of multiple small-scale alternative values that we can identify as the middle city.

The urban cultures

'Middle city' is a term that can quite conveniently be used to give a qualitative definition to culture as well as to a city. Defined in the developing world as the informal city by Arif Hasan, this is the urban culture that characteristically must negotiate with the formal culture and is therefore reluctant to codify and place constraints on its options. We can use the phrase meso-culture (Khosla 2002) from the Greek word *mesos* meaning middle. The counterpoint to middle is macro. The macro-city is the dominant city, the city in the imagination of Haussmann, the city of codified rules and written regulations and the receptacle of the dominant written culture. A compassionate city needs to blend two aspects of urban living – the static physical and the kinetic perceptual aspects. The static physical aspect is its macro aspect, an aspect that could be regarded as the realm of the literati where the civic order of its institutions has been codified into a series of written rules and regulations.

The dynamism of the life of the city, on the other hand, is provided by the interaction between the static and the kinetic components of the city. It is this interaction that spurs the development process in the city. Inevitably the static components are put under pressure by the kinetic elements. As in

Colonial centre
around Sula Paya
pagoda, Yangon,
Myanmar
(Rangoon,
Burma).

Jeremy (Horner/
Panos)

Macro-city urban culture

Static
Dominant physical structure
Written culture
Codified civic order
Rules and regulations
Established institutions

Old Delhi, India.

(Chris Stowers/
Panos)

Middle-city urban culture

Kinetic
Temporary stability and spontaneous arrangements
Spoken culture
No written civil code of order
Acceptance of diversity
Carnivals and ethnic celebrations

all macro-urban cultures, the written rules are and need to be resisted by the pressures of the emergent, ever-changing relationships and initiatives that arise from the collaborations and negotiations of citizens interacting and adjusting to each other in the realm of the oral, unwritten kinetic domain. These are the domains where folk cultures express their relatively spontaneous initiatives and dynamism.

The kinetic component of the city is essentially of temporary stability, mediating its spaces and forms between the pressures of the micro-world of the citizens and the macro-city world of established institutions and civic order, written rules and regulations and the imposition of state law on city regulation. The kinetic component of the city constitutes the world of spoken culture, of carnivals, ethnic celebrations and processions – a world that is reluctant to codify its civic order into written rules and regulations. Here the community meshes its activities not along functional regulations but on the basis of a permissiveness bordering on the turbulence of a moving stream; where tolerance and acceptability of the ensuing chaos is almost an asset to use and exploit in new, dynamic and ever-shifting ways.

Citizens of a middle city, or mesocity, define their cultural, economic and social identities through their interaction with the dominant macro-city. A city as a whole could therefore be viewed as a domain, a territory, a region where two inner cities co-exist – the macro-city and the middle city. Each of these cities relates to the other and needs to be side by side. The boundaries between the two are fuzzy and need to remain so. There is not a city in this world where these two vital components are not supporting each other and yet, more often than not, the dominant macro-city is perpetually trying to obliterate its middle half because it perceives the middle city as a threat to its ideal and its identity. The administration of the macro-city which believes in a written civic order actively resists the middle city, generally insisting on converting what are essentially folk festivals and celebrations into its civilized dimensions and moral order. The macro-city bulldozes and codifies ethnic cultures and replaces these with written macro-moral order and municipal dictates. The inhabitants of the middle city thus have the greatest constraints on their freedom.

We need to understand that the economy of the city can become dynamic with the interaction of the two inner cities in a special interdependent relationship. In many Third World cities – for example, Mumbai or Karachi – the majority of inhabitants live in the domain of the meso-culture, even though they may occupy marginal lands. It is these inhabitants who provide the greatest opportunities for initiating development because they are the un-free with potentials far beyond their opportunities and rights. In order to include them in the process of city dynamics one needs to include them in the idea and identity of the city.

The dynamics in the life of any city, be it from the post-industrial west or the underdeveloped Third World, is triggered by what sociologists Robert Redfield and Milton Singer describe as the characteristics of city parts:

> *"populated by people of diverse cultural origins removed from their indigenous seats of cultures. They are cities in which new states of mind, following from these characteristics are developed and become prominent. The new states of mind are indifferent to or inconsistent with, or supersede or overcome, states of mind associated with local cultures and ancient civilizations. The individuals of these ... cities, if any, are the intelligentsia rather than the literati."*

Redfield and Singer (1954)

The garden city

We mentioned earlier that the idealization of the city took two entirely different routes. We can clearly see the significance of both these routes by observing the effects of these routes on the quality of life of the inhabitants of the middle city. The first example chose to regularize the city with rules and regulations best exemplified by Haussmann's work. We now come to the other route – the ideal garden city, a reflection of paradise set in the countryside. This model was essentially socialist in its concerns, trying to provide the middle city with a level of certain humanism that would enable its inhabitants to adjust more gently to the trauma of migration and home building in an alien environment. Like the proponents of regularization, the garden city was planned on the assumption of a higher moral order that enabled the workers to live in harmony with nature and industry. The garden city advocates, like the proponents of regularization, had adopted the same nineteenth century assumptions that Darwin had confirmed, specifying the natural orders of superiority that were applied to class and culture.

The contributions to this ideal were probably first made by the anarchist Prince Peter Kropotkin, a geographer who first put forward his ideas in his book called *Fields, Factories and Workshops* (1899) and in his earlier work, *Should We Concern Ourselves with the Ideal Society of the Future* (1873). Stites (1989) describes Kropotkin's depiction of a new Russia as a freely formed federation of self-governing peasant communities in full ownership and possession of the land as a common community asset to be distributed equally. All urban property was to be owned by the peasant and the institution of higher learning was to be converted to craft and trade-based schools (Mumford 1961). Some of his ideas were taken up by the Englishmen Ebenezer Howard and Robert Owen both of whom translated them into physical proposals without the revolutionary assumptions.

For Ebenezer Howard, the garden city was a place where there existed 'the splendid possibilities of a new civilization based on service to the community'. The big overcrowded city was regarded by Howard as a self-defeating proposition. In his book *Garden Cities of Tomorrow* (1902), he propagated not a revolutionary concept but a classical one based on Greek ideas of urban settlements limited in size.

The untitled city

Both these routes leading to the idealization of the city, either through regularization or the garden city, necessarily assumed a large degree of coercion. The regularization ideal was based on physical demolition and forceful occupation of the urban space occupied by the middle city. The garden city ideal assumed a gentler form of coercion by which the workers were not physically removed form the city but were settled in production units established by industrial entrepreneurs. Some of these models were built by the chocolate barons in Bourneville, England and in the Krupp industrialist colonies in Essen, Germany. The nature of coercions in urban living styles and values has continued to be a part of the architectural development imagination in the twentieth century. For example, Le Cobusier's model for the centre of Paris in 1930 combined a Haussmann-like approach with the ideals of the Garden Movement.

Ideals have a powerful influence on those who have historically been responsible for determining the formations of cities. However, the effect of imposed social restrictions inherent in the physical planning of cities has like-wise been responsible for a detrimental subjugation of the quality of life of those inhabitants of the middle city. The majority of these citizens experience great obstructions to leading the life they value. These citizens consequently provide the greatest opportunities for initiating development because they are the unfree with potentials far beyond their opportunities and rights. With the widening of the democratic process and the emphasis on sustainable urban development, we can now put forward the ideals of Amartya Sen and his vital concerns in removing unfreedoms. Unfreedoms are the specific constraints, impositions and coercions to the individual citizen's capabilities. Removing these obstructions enables citizens living in communities to expand their lives with measures that they value. Therefore the functioning of cities and good governance can be radically transformed by applying Sen's ideal of a continuous human development policy specifically directed to those inhabitants of middle city. Modified urban development policies would be guided by the objective of ever-expanding freedom and the improvement of the human condition.

- 2 -

New Patterns of Urbanization

We observe our world caught up in a fast moving process of urbanization that is unprecedented in the history of urban settlements. Huge demographic movements are taking place in Africa and Asia at this moment. Millions of people are being displaced by the ravages of armed conflicts, arbitrary authoritarianism and the absence of governance. The displaced are migrating to urban centres and very soon we will have to accept that more people on this globe will be living in cities than in the countryside. In the past 20 years, more than a dozen mega-cities have appeared and an urban population of 10 million is not uncommon. If estimates in *The Economist* (9 May 2002) are to be believed in the next decade an extra 100 million people will join the cities of Africa and 340 million in the cities of Asia: equivalent of a new Bangkok every two months. By 2030, nearly two-thirds of the world, population will be urban.

If we combine the effect of this enormous migration with the contention of the World Bank that the number of poor is increasing, cities have surely become the places from which the directions for new development policies must emerge.

It could be argued that this rush to the city from the countryside is part of a historical process that had already been experienced by the west at the end of the industrial revolution. But there are important differences. These differences could have significant implications for current policy formulations that are intended to support economic development in the developing world. Consider these differences:

- Many parts of the developing world are without effective central authority.

- The migration to the towns is not only economic, but also in part caused by push factors related to the growing chaos and insecurity in the countryside.

- There is little evidence of significant investment in urban infrastructure that could absorb this influx of urban population. Unlike at the time of the industrial revolution when the enormous rise in factory production and investment offered jobs to the urban migrants, today's developing world migrants often have few employment opportunities that would result in value being added to the economy. On the contrary often this migration gives rise to hidden unemployment.

- There is either an absence of representative authority or the presence of weak state structures.

- Effective intervention often takes the form of an imposed military presence.

- The identity of the nation state is being compromised by increasingly militant expressions of regional or ethnic identities that are centred on territorial claims. These claims often cleanse regions from ethnic groups by forcing them to migrate.

- These conditions are prevalent not only in many parts of the developing world but also in large parts of the former Soviet Union territories which once had high levels of industrialization.

The historical precedence is therefore reminiscent not so much of the post-industrial experience of the west as it is of other periods in the history of Europe. Eric Hobsbawm explains:

"I believe that the disintegration of the states in these regions of the world is mainly the result of the collapse of the colonial empires, of the end of the era in which the great European powers controlled large portions of the world, where they had found non-state governed societies, and had imposed a degree of external and internal order. This also applies to the territories conquered by Russia after 1800, such as the Caucasus ... What has occurred in these parts of the world seems to be similar in some ways to what occurred in Western Europe following the fall of the Roman Empire. There was no longer any central authority. In some cases there were local authorities, which still managed to function, in other cases there was conquest by groups from outside which came to establish order. However, in reality vast regions of Europe lacked normal and permanent state structures for a long period of time. I believe that this is occurring again in parts of the world."

Hobsbawm, 2000

Urgency for new urban-based initiatives

The motivation for this sudden spurt in urban migration in many parts of the developed world is not just a move towards greater job opportunities but more significantly it is a move that includes a search for greater security from the growing social and economic disorder in the countryside. Thus the search for solutions needs to weigh the choices between rural and urban-based development initiatives. It is clear that development policies need to urgently address the lack of adequate state authority in order to secure development initiatives. Weak state authorities need to be strengthened. State authorities are located in cities to enable them to affect control. Their presence would therefore make it imperative to focus the primary thrust of development initiatives in the urban centres. If the growing anarchy of the countryside is to be effectively tackled, it will need to be tackled by the urban-based state authority. Such an authority would need to be strengthened through urban-based development initiatives and programmes.

The need to strengthen urban-based state authorities is a precondition to establishing a sense of order in the country as a whole. The growing disorder in the countryside needs urban-based remedies. However, the need to bolster up the capacities of state administrations cannot presume that strong urban-based rule is per se acceptable without qualitative conditions. A strong urban-based non-democratic dictatorial regime, for instance, would not be conducive to development. Although such a regime could be seen as a strong counter-force to stateless disorder, its very definition as an undemocratic system of governance precludes it from being development-friendly. Such regimes introduce arbitrary military priorities that often counter people-friendly development goals with harrowing consequences for the people – as is the case with the man-made famine in Sudan. There is ample analysis supporting the importance of participatory policies in development theories to demonstrate that elected friendly governance is a pre-requisite to successful and lasting urban development.

Freedoms for cities

There can be little doubt why Sen has re-examined the process of cooperate participation policies in the lives of those who inhabit the mega-cities. For Sen, cities are extraordinarily important and the nature of the unfreedoms must be recognized and removed if the higher aims of human development are to be made equally possible for all citizens. On the method of implementing his ideals for global urban governance goals he cites three concerns to advise those formulating policy.[7]

First, in Sen's view cities have very peculiar problems and unfreedoms. By way of illustration, he gave the example of a woman giving birth in a city hospital might be less prone to die due to a complicated delivery than in a village hospital if the latter lacks specialized equipment or specialist doctors. This is a freedom gained for urban citizens. On the other hand, Sen explained that in these circumstances:

"dense cities have increased health problems as experienced through the spread of contagions and ecological pollutants in the air and water. The city may lack sufficient civic amenities, as in Calcutta where one quarter of the population of the entire state lives in one city. Creating and maintaining schools with populations of this scale is a huge task."

In this respect there are many types of unfreedoms particular to the mega-cities. Determining the specific characteristics of the unfreedoms and those most vulnerable can only be understood through conferring with the individuals and the community.

Second, in his words there appears to be an almost fatalistic attitude to the future of cities. The more he refers to urban development literature, the more he observes there are those who predict the growth of mega-cities as an inevitable consequence:

"For example, they do not ask the question 'Will Calcutta grow to 16 million or not?' They simple say that it will. Surely these are matters for us to decide. I don't mean we can decide to enforce planning regulations that will restrict urbanization and therefore, Calcutta or Rio will not grow any further. We could start with the understanding that cities grow because certain types of facilities are available and not elsewhere. And then we would recognize that the unfreedoms of a city are chosen in exchange for the unfreedoms of non-city life."

For Sen, the predictions of inevitable growth of our mega-cities misread the human capability – which is in the domain of human freedoms – into something of an inescapable need of a modern economy. He believes we have the freedom to do something: 'It is not a question of a meteor that is going to hit us about which we would want to do something but can do nothing but wait for the impact.' Sen explains that it is a question of deciding the action of city planning. Urban policy would need to change the incentive structure that lays bare the formation of city growth. As long as we adhere to the old fashioned centralized planning he does not think we will be successful. Questions need to be raised as to what freedoms we have to redefine the nature of development. As development takes place we need to question what freedoms we have to run cities better? If we determine what kind of broad pattern the society wants, we must question what are the ways in which the relative gap in the attraction to the city can be reduced.In his view, the mega-cities are not inescapable parts of living in the modern age. The central challenge is to see that we have many more freedoms to create the future and arrange atmospheres in which these unfreedoms can be avoided.

Third, if we want to have smaller cities, Sen believes this is not a matter for the government to control, but surely a freedom for the people to choose. What is needed for any of these processes to be effective is the commitment to identify obstructions to the individual's ability to take part in the social decision-making process. Transparency guarantees, for example, will provide accurate information and allow people to think intelligently so that the right questions will be posed. Only then will a participatory process be effective. These decisions are an intrinsic part of the organization of society. One of the most central issues we must decide is where to locate ourselves within the rural–urban spectrum of human settlements.

> *"Here is the opportunity to view the unfreedom of the city balanced against the freedom of the human being living in society to choose the kind of world they want in which the mega-cities are up for contention."*
>
> *Sen, LSE Colloquium*

Sen explained that in these circumstances policy makers will continue to make mistakes if the primary focus continues to look at economic issues and just getting jobs to determine the economic sustainability and attraction to cities. He advised one has to find out more about why these locational choices are made. Then we can consider how we actually bring about the change and follow through with the principles of participation when determining the right incentive. It would not be adequate, in Sen's opinion, if the government discovers people do not want a mega-city and then implements that choice through clamping down regulations. The process of implementation has to be a participatory process too.

Sen stressed that clearly civic society is more active now; there is more media coverage and therefore there is more public interest and discussion. The public is taking a greater interest in a wide range of human development concerns. There are many more people thinking on these issues. He believes these public discussions must be seen as a continuous process where there is a lot more that can be done. We must use whatever participation now exists and expand that level even further. Sen asks us to look closely at the real mechanisms that are linked with the success of the participation process and the political process of democracy. The determining factor in almost every instance relies on the media support. He gave the example of Pakistan:

> *"I think one of the real joys and glories of civic society is in Pakistan where there are now a number of newspapers. This is a phenomenon that did not exist until quite recently. Some of these reporters in the media have taken enormous risks and were arrested under the previous government. There are so many courageous journalists and many times what blocks them is not their willingness to stand up to authoritarian governments, it is financial difficulties in running their papers. On the one side there is an enormous willingness of human beings to stand up and be counted and do their work in participation. On the other side*

News stand in
Peshawar,
Pakistan.

(Piers Benatar/
Panos)

*trivial sums of money can stop these things at the fraction of the cost that
goes into large industry. Consider the situation with the media world, in
contrast to the large sums of money involved with commerce and industry. It could be dramatically different. It is appalling there are so little
funds support media coverage when we consider the value of human life
– the scarcest of all these things. People are willing to give their lives –
and stand up and risk imprisonment, death and torture. This determination is available in great measure, which is a great tribute to the view
of human beings as the quintessential agents of change."*

Sen's contention is that the development process is inextricably bound
up with a process of ever expanding freedoms that need to be granted to
the individuals of a community. In enhancing the capabilities and potentials of the citizens of an urban society, or for that matter any society, policy
makers need to focus on areas that will give the greatest impact. Not only
is there a need for the greatest impact, there is also the need to intervene
in those areas where the multiplier effect of the consequent benefits will be
the greatest. The impact of urban development initiatives will spread the
significant benefits to all un-free communities.

> *"I think the unfreedoms experienced in many cities across the world
> look in the abstract viciously difficult but it may not be quite like that
> as things change slowly. The problem is how to move to the next step
> – once you are there it is not a hard thing to run. The challenge is the
> change, the shift and if you are changing over time you could do it. But
> it has to be done with more intelligence more humanity and more
> participation."* [7]

- 3 -

Amartya Sen and Enlarging Development Policy

In their citation announcement for the 1998 award of the Nobel Prize in Economic Science, The Royal Swedish Academy mentioned that: 'By combining tools from economics and philosophy, Sen had restored an ethical dimension to the discussion of vital economic problems'. His work, *Development as Freedom* is both philosophical as well as a treatise on economics. By combining the principle concerns of economics with the ethical questions of philosophy, he has opened up a new domain, which is far more comprehensive than the hitherto more popular independent domains confined to the discipline of economics. The two key words in the title of the book separately form a subject of vast information, research and theories. The topic of development is a vast enterprise, as is freedom. By combining these two enterprises into a correlated whole, he has achieved a sort of fission effect that reveals new ways to move forward toward improving the human condition in this new post-ideological age.

Sen has advocated the need to re-evaluate the framework of development to encompass a much wider concept that centres on freedom rather than on a debate about poverty versus prosperity. New parameters are defined that include an expanded definition of development. There is an assumption that development integrates economic, social and political considerations with equal weight. However, the traditional narrower economic strategies had an almost exclusive focus on economic criteria to the detriment of human development values. These earlier and narrower criteria tended to subjugate the social and political aspects and regard them as less important than economic aspects. Governments could justify undemocratic, exploitative or repressive regimes to achieve high growth rates.

The role of the government

In the middle of the twentieth century, the realities of the cold war provoked extensive academic debate on how alternative economic and social systems could improve the human condition. This debate was centred on how the so-called factors of production – land, labour and capital – could be combined in the best way possible to increase the wealth of nations. Marx had introduced the notion of the need to wrest control of these factors of production from private ownership and place them in public ownership. The liberal and pro-capitalist economists formulated theoretical alternatives to demonstrate that private ownership of these factors could provide a better alternative to the communist planned economies. These contesting theories of economic growth were intensified in the midst of decolonization. As large parts of the world became independent, the new leaders began to look for ways to improve their wealth and prosperity. In searching for these ways, they had to choose between two alternative models of economic growth – one the Soviet and Chinese models of post-revolutionary society, and the other the American model of private enterprise.

The role of the state in development

The depression of the 1930s and the significant role that Keynesian policies played in mitigating its worse consequences had confirmed that the state needed to play an important role in supporting development. The downward spiral of lack of demand, leading to a lack of investment, leading to massive unemployment, in turn leading to further reduction in demand, needed to be broken. This break could only be introduced by macro-level state interventions as classical economics solely relying on market mechanisms could not deliver. The Marshall Plan for the reconstruction of Europe firmly established the proactive role of the state in economic affairs as a balancing force to market mechanisms. Many new independent nations followed policies of state intervention in their economic programmes. Keynesian doctrine, as well as the experience of the Soviet Union, endorsed, at varying degree, the economic responsibilities of the state. Borrowing the terminology of the soviets, India, for example, adopted the instrument of the five-year plan to direct social investments.

Early development theories advocating a rush towards industrialization and take-off (best seen in Rostow 1960) were postulated as alternatives to the Soviet model that had industrialized at a phenomenal rate. Such approaches saw development as an aggressive process that was fierce and tough and contested the socialist view of development, which was that development was pre-conditioned by traumatic revolution. Opposing views on development engaged the two power blocks in a contest for constituency gains in the poor world. Both power blocks poured aid into the developing world to support vast capital-intensive infrastructure projects. There were enormous and undeniable gains from these investments, but the solution to poverty eradication remained elusive.

Centre for Alternative Technology
Canolfan y Dechnoleg Amgen
Machynlleth, Powys SY20 9AZ
Tel. 01654 705950 www.cat.org.uk

Dear Customer,

We are delighted to enclose our Winter Collection for 2011. Inside you'll find handy and practical household solutions – everything from bamboo underwear to the most up-to-date renewable energy books available.

This is just a small taster of the much larger range we have online in our EcoStore at http://store.cat.org.uk/ UK Mainland Online Orders over £40.00 are carriage free!

Please feel free to get in contact if you have a particular title you are searching for or a subject area you are interested in and we will do our very best to help you.

Many thanks for your continued support of our work here at CAT,

Best Wishes

The CAT Ecostore

ANNE SCHIFFER
FLAT 9, HAMILTON HOUSE
TRAFALGAR STREET
LEEDS
YORKSHIRE
LS2 7BF   21805/382 A 426

**If undelivered please return to
CAT, Machynlleth, Powys, SY20 9AZ**

How to order:

Fully complete the order form and add postage from the chart.

Phone us on 01654 705959
email: **mail.order@cat.org.uk**
Post: **CAT, Mail Order, Machynlleth, Powys, SY20 9AZ**
For our full range of products and more about CAT, see
http://store.cat.org.uk

Name

Address   Delivery Address if Different

Postcode: Postcode:
Daytime Telephone Number:
E mail:

I enclose a cheque payable to CAT plc ☐   Please charge my credit/debit card ☐

Card No.

Issue No.   Expiry Date: Valid From Date:

Signature

Due to new credit card security measures, if you are paying by card, we will need to phone you on receipt of your order to obtain your security code. Please make sure you have provided a daytime telephone number to enable us to call you and for us to send out your order promptly. We may send you other relevant mailings from CAT Charity or CAT plc or their trading subsidiaries (we will never pass your details to any outside organisations). Please tick here if you do not wish to receive any other CAT mailings ☐

2011 Postage Rates

UK Mainland Only
Goods up to £12.00 add £2.95
Goods £12.01 and over add £4.95

Highlands and Islands, Northern Ireland, Isle of Man & Scilly Isles, Guernsey & Jersey
Goods up to £12.00 add £2.95
Goods between £12.01-£39.99 add £4.95
Goods over £40.00 to non UK Mainland areas above, please contact us to discuss the most favourable postage method and price.

Item/Description	Qty.	Price	Total
Goods total			£
Add postage from chart			£
Donation to CAT Charity Ltd. (Charity No 265239) Thank you!			£
TOTAL			£

In the second half of the twentieth century, theories of economic development in the democratic world continued to evolve. This evolution was partly in response to the mixed choices that many developing countries had made about their routes to economic prosperity. For instance India, Egypt and Ghana chose to opt for non-aligned, non-revolutionary policies that combined socialist planning with state protected private enterprise. Development economists needed to consider the constraints that arose from the varying choices of economic growth models made by post-colonial countries. Despite considerable improvements in the economic status of these developing countries, and despite half a century of searching for solutions, national wealth continued to be eroded by the persistence of devastating poverty.

The impact of the cold war

The issue of 'continuous development' as a broad goal for the improvement of the human condition has always been placed within an area of concern that lies equidistant between the disciplines of economics and philosophy. In the twentieth century however, this issue seems to have dominated the field of economics more than the field of philosophy. This is understandable since great strides had been made in the theoretical formulations that have informed the realm of economics. The establishment of the Soviet Union expanded the theoretical formulations of Marxism as a defined alternative economic system. Across the ideological divide, equally large strides were taken in the theoretical body of thought that proposed free enterprise as a solution to the predicaments of continuous development.

The cold war profoundly affected the discipline and literature of economics as it influenced so much else. The whole issue of human rights came to the fore. The confrontation of the cold war polarized the criteria for achieving improvements in the human condition. On one hand, the west accused the socialist countries of having a poor record on human rights while, on the other, the socialist countries accused the west of tolerating poverty and deprivation as the evils of the market system. Both ideologies were in agreement that a process of development was required and that it needed fiscal investments. But the two sides always answered the eternal philosophical question of justifications and 'ends and means' in diametrically opposite ways. Indeed these opposite views were clearly apparent in the contrasting ways and means of raising and spending fiscal investments in development. The two sides in the cold war were thus not only military adversaries but also philosophical, economical and moral adversaries. The formalized collapse of the socialist project in the past decade has brought about fundamental changes in the future potentials of the measures and goals of development. Both ideologies had expressed their achievements in contesting measurable indicators of the economy, often related to the levels of industrialization.

Fifty years of contesting with the Soviet Union had affected liberal core attitudes and policies toward both developed and underdeveloped communities. In rejecting the centrally planned economy approach, liberal attitudes advocated development through decentralized, unplanned economies that could be reliant on the market mechanism and the spirit of private enterprise. The achievements and successes of both approaches were measured and evaluated by a range of indices that emphasized the measurement of economic prosperity as represented by national income. Thus average per capita income levels, national income, gross national product (GNP), level of industrialization, percentage of urban population, literacy levels, etc. provided seemingly convincing criteria for the comparison of the development levels of a community or a country. The two contesting systems used these indicators to gauge the relative merits and successes of each ideological system. Such criteria facilitated comparison of the status of societies across the ideological divide. And, because data from these indices was cumulative across a time span, it became possible to compare the trajectories of development that a society had achieved under each ideological system.

The twenty-first century began with a sense of triumph for the liberal democratic system. The Freedom Approach to development has been vindicated as opposed to the anti-Freedom Approach of the Soviet system. There are now new opportunities available to widen the focus to include more fundamental philosophical issues that relate to the real goals of development. No longer are the criteria for levels of development constrained by the need to compare and contest the duality of the economic ideologies of the past century. While new and variant ideologies may continue to emerge and fade, the discipline of economics can now return to some of its early concerns about the nature of the human condition in free societies.

The new climate

The neo-liberal shift of the early 1980s and the collapse of the socialist project in the 1990s has modified the future options for economic growth models for the developing world. In the present uni-polar world of Pax–Americana, it is no longer possible for countries to promote models of mixed economies. Globalization and economic liberalism have dismantled the national edifices of socially owned resources. The goals of economic growth have been tempered with the conditionality of good governance and the free market. For instance, in the Balkans, the adjustment that was forced onto Bulgaria by the international financial institutions led to massive problems. Hyper-inflation of 1330 per cent in 1997, high unemployment of anything up to 50 per cent and a disintegrating social safety net led to widespread disillusionment. This in an industrial country and yet by the turn of the twenty-first century, the Ministry of Social Welfare estimated that 80 per cent of the population was living below the poverty line. While the World Bank and the European Union moved in to solve the macro problems which they were certainly help to aggravate, new emphasis began to emerge on the problems of post-industrial countries. The whole debate about the merits of rural-led versus urban-led development needs to be reconsidered as the options for economic investments are being redefined.

The emphasis began to shift considerably from an almost exclusive focus on macro issues towards sophisticated approaches that address micro-level intervention. New hope needed to percolate down to the population. With the growing importance of the work of worldwide NGOs, policy makers have begun to be better informed about micro sectors. This has resulted in a growing understanding of the nature of poverty and its many dimensions. Policy directives and identification of goals and targets have widened considerably and social investment has become a crucial component of economic investment.

In this new climate, arguments about economic development that had been ideologically rooted in attaining greater wealth have been replaced with emphasis on human development. Inspired by the work of social anthropology and grass-roots endeavours, newer models have been constructed around more focused issues such as urban poverty, sustainable futures, rights to information, decentralized democracy, gender issues, cultural sensitivities, healthcare, etc. International donors, influenced by the UNDP Human Developments Reports, have begun to re-evaluate the goals of their aid programmes and take on board the strategies for a people-centred approach.

The just society

At the beginning of the new century, it can perhaps be said that the highest goal of a society's achievement is to enable its individuals to be able to live in a free society. Since the beginnings of economics and earlier, writers have been discussing the qualities that such a free society should consent to. Traditional philosophical concerns about the goals of seeking a just human society can be considered as a combination of a number of approaches. Among the more important ones is 'utilitarianism' which focuses on seeking a sense of satisfaction or happiness achieved through the acquisition of utility goods in as much as they fulfil one's desires. Such an approach does not consider the importance of the value of freedom or the nature of the distribution of the goods and happiness amongst the commu-

Ex-child labourers
in Mongolia
protest against
the exploitation of
children.

(Fernando
Moleres/
Panos)

nity. The need to have recognized rights does not feature as a desirable goal. Thus an unjust society is one that is unhappier than it should be and the measurement of this unhappiness might indicate what needs to be done to rectify the situation. The other ideas about a just society define, with various intensities, the importance of liberty. 'Libertarianism' preoccupies itself with liberties and rights of different kinds. Satisfaction and happiness are not regarded as important. Thus having rights of freedom, the right to own property, civil rights, etc are considered an absolute necessity. Social goals have no priority in this view of a just society. The proponents of these ideas each put forward different ways to evaluate what they considered to be the goal of social stability.

Current paradigms of poverty reduction and social justice have evolved from these earlier ideas. However the original concerns to seek ways to form just societies remain pivotal to most development theories. Many subjective, qualitative and relative approaches aiming to incorporate the individual agent in the evaluation of poverty have been proposed since the late 1970s. The better ones include the Human Development Index tailored by the UNDP, Amartya Sen's entitlement perspective representing poverty as a failure to access resources, and a social anthropological notion of vulnerability as relating to poverty from which came the Sustainable Livelihoods approach of Robert Chambers, now backed by UK's DFID.

All these alternatives have in common an attempt at comprehending poverty in its complexity, diversity and subjectivity. The use of participatory means help to convey alternative people-centred views of the cause of poverty. The poor cease to be seen as a monolithic, static and impersonal group of individuals but come to be considered as agents of change, not recipients in, but accelerators of, the development process.

The individual as the agent of change

From a perspective that ideologically regarded the individual as the unit of society, Sen's recasting of the priorities of a Freedom Approach to development has reinforced the pivotal role of the individual in any development strategy. The individual is seen as the accelerator of potential change. The individual potentials and character are the components which make possible their unique capability to lead the life they value leading. The more unrealized the individual's potentials; the lower is their level of development. Sen's redefined Freedom Approach describes the processes of development as a quest by individuals for ever-expanding freedom to live the life they value leading. Previously economic criteria for evaluating development consisted of measuring GNP, personal incomes, levels of industrialisation and so on. While these continue to remain valid for evaluation, they are now seen only as a means to expand freedom and not as an ends.

While there are many freedom constraints that are shared by the community as common obstructions, the freeing of these common obstructions does not relieve the individuals of the community from their unfreedoms. This new approach considers each citizen, their capability and potential, as an independent agent of change.

The individual and the collective

In discussion with Amartya Sen and Lord Meghnad Desai at the London School of Economics, concerns regarding the relationship of the individual to the collective were raised by a representative from the NGO SPARC. (SPARC supports the National Slum Dwellers Federation in Mumbai, India). Celine D'cruz explained how in their work they believed it is collective behaviour which helps the slum dwellers achieve individual empowerment in getting ration cards, housing or securing tenure. Sen agreed that individual freedom in this case is enhanced by the social collective action and that is the way to look at it. However, one must distinguish between what is to be achieved, individual freedom or collective action? It does not make any sense to have a worshipping of society that it is not related to the individual. For example: "It would be absurd to say no one's life is going to be better, but it is a better society. If society is better then in some way somebody's life must be getting better." [8] According to Sen, the fact that one cannot address the freedoms of individual lives without having social changes, social institutions, social cooperation and the kind of activates SPARC supports, does not undervalue the importance of individual freedom.

Sen referred to Marx as 'the great individualist' who had some very interesting things to say on the subject of the individual and the collective. In Sen's first book, a mathematical work, *Choice of Techniques*, Sen begins with a quotation from Marx on the front page: 'what has to be avoided, above all, is viewing the individual as alienated from society and also viewing society as alienated from the individual.' The point is that when we consider the entire progression of Sen's ideals as a social development economist, we must look at the individual in the society.

At the same meeting at LSE Lord Meghnad Desai mapped a more historic definition that has changed over time:

> "It is not to do with individualistic in the sense of a certain eighteenth or nineteenth century thinking but individualistic at a higher level, to use an old fashioned expression. The idea is not that the individual only matters and there is no such thing as society. It's more the fact that if one does not value the individuals within a collectivity, very often a collectivity can be extremely repressive. Women especially have experienced how the notion of community can be used in a very oppressive way indeed. Therefore we have to ask, how do we get into a better level of individual collectivity intervention which is liberating?"'

While exploring the freedom of individuals within gender roles in the late 1960s and early 1970s, Sen looked at the inequality within the family in all kinds of ways including what leads to high mortality rates and lack of nutrition and so on. A response he received from a colleague at the Delhi School of Economics in the cultural anthropology department criticized him for using the wrong concepts. He was told: 'the Indian woman does not have an understanding for the individual, she has concepts only of the family'. For Sen the understanding of the individual was what made equality possible and the absence of it allowed the inequality to survive. The concept of the individual as distinct – but not unrelated to the family was an enormously important part of the liberation they were trying to work towards.

"So it is a great achievement, partly because the world has changed, partly we have all changed, partly because we have discovered a variety of things about the human condition.

We have refocused ourselves not on the state, although the state is rather important, we have focused back on the individual. It is not an individual listing doctrine that Amartya has put forward, rather it is the individual connected with collectivity. At the same time the collectivity, on the one hand is enabling, but for many, many people it is also an adversity. We are older and perhaps if not wiser and we have seen that collectivities which were not democratic and fully participating are not good collectivities. The fact they are either sanctioned by tradition or doctrine or religion or whatever, it's not a sufficient reason to live with them.

It is liberating that we go back to the individual, focus on the individual, and ask yourself what are the unfreedoms that we can cure."

Lord Meghnad Desai, LSE ColloquiumJuly 2003

Part II

Obstructions to Urban Development

- 4 -

Five Freedoms

The constraints and obstructions to ever-expanding freedoms are termed 'unfreedoms' – barriers that could exist in the economic, social or political realms of society. Thus poverty, malnutrition, poor sanitation, tyranny, poor economic opportunities, social deprivations, poor public facilities, intolerance, communalisation, ethnic centricity, repressive state apparatuses, lack of education, absence of healthcare, lack of security and corruption can all be termed unfreedoms. They are all regarded as equally relevant.

In the efforts to remove unfreedoms, vital roles are played by markets, market-related organizations, governments, local authorities, political parties, civic institutions, educational facilities and media. Removing unfreedoms will provide opportunities for free speech and public debate on social norms and values about childcare, gender issues as well as the treatment of the environment. There is a need for a multi-objective strategy to remove the obstructions. In evaluating the degree of freedom available to the individuals of a society or community, the citizen's rights and opportunities are perceived through the perspective of five different and distinct components of freedom: political freedoms, economics facilities, social opportunities, transparency guarantees and protective security.

Removing unfreedoms

- Champions the individual citizen as societies most important component.
- The process of development is one that removes obstructions and enables the citizen to move closer to the life that he or she values.
- Freedom can be expanded through specific policies that consider the five components or instruments that influence the potential and character of the individual citizen.
- These are the instruments that citizens need to enable them to overcome their constraints. More importantly these are the instruments that inform us of the degree of obstructions that are prevalent in a society, and hence the degree of underdevelopment.

Aung San Suu Kyi, Nobel Peace Prize Laureate and General Secretary of the National League for Democracy, delivering her regular Saturday speech to the general public outside her home. Yangon, Myanmar (Rangoon, Burma).

(Dean Chapman/ Panos)

It is the simplicity and totality of attaining ever-expanding freedom through this development approach that merits our special attention. The five instruments of freedom define comprehensive, universal, moral and ethical principles relevant to our current circumstances and goals for urban development policy These instruments are the principle means of accessing the rights and opportunities that citizens need to enable them to overcome their obstructions. The obstructions can be clearly identified and expanded through these interdependent development tools. The five freedoms tools are like the filters through which one can evaluate the level of development of an individual, a household, or a community, a city or a nation. Ideally a freedom index framework would be devised for micro and macro observations and determine the constraints and obstructions to those citizens of the middle city. These five instruments of freedom are explained as the following.

Political freedoms

The free opportunities citizens have to determine who should govern them and on what principles. Enshrined in this opportunity is the right to evaluate and criticize authorities, to a free press as well as freedom of expression and participation in the political process. During the twentieth century, various forms of undemocratic governments behaved in brutal ways that have severely damaged the prospects of development in their countries. Abuses of human rights – in Myanmar, to take one example – have placed significant constraints on human freedom and hence human development. But despite the presence of these autocratic regimes, significant progress has been made at a global level. The UN informs us of this progress. While in 1975 only 33 countries had ratified the 'International Covenant on Civil and Political Rights'; this figure had risen to 144 by 2000. In 1900 no country had universal suffrage while today almost all countries have it. Between 1974 and 1999, multiparty election systems had been introduced in 113 more countries and today only about 40 countries do not have multiparty electoral systems.

Economic facilities

Inhabitants need to have the opportunities and freedom to use the economic resources of the city, its hinterland and other territories for the purposes of consumption, production and exchange (trade). Freedom of access to these facilities includes the availability and access to finance potential opportunities. Being able to gain a productive livelihood through the means of one's choice requires adequate and supportive facilities. The lack of such facilities is an unfreedom and a constraint to development. At

A woman shows her identity card as she queues to cast her vote in the 2004 South African election.

(Sven Torfinn/ Panos)

least 150 million of the world's workers were unemployed at the end of 1998. The causes of unemployment can vary within a society and may be caused by social constraints – for instance, in South Africa, the unemployment rate for African males is seven times higher than that of their white counterparts. Apart from the unemployment of the workforce, in developing countries, there are some 250 million child labourers.

Social opportunities

The arrangements and choice of opportunities that the administration makes for education, healthcare and other essential community facilities for its citizens is relevant to evaluate the level of development. It is an essential responsibility of the administration to provide opportunities for the basic requirements of its inhabitants and not leave these to undefined national agencies. Much progress has undoubtedly been achieved. Between 1980 and 1999, malnutrition was reduced and the proportion of underweight children in the underdeveloped world fell by 10 per cent to 27 per cent. Between 1970 and 1999, in the rural areas of the developing world, the percentage of people with access to safe water increased fourfold to 71 per cent. But severe deprivations remain worldwide: 1.2 billion people still live on less than US$1.00 a day, and 2.4 billion people lack sanitation facilities.

Girls sit three to a desk at a newly opened girl's high school, Afghanistan.

Karen Robinson/ Panos)

Transparency guarantees

Citizens need to be provided with the guarantees of openness, necessary disclosures and rights to information as well as tangible evidence of trust so that the clauses of the social contract between the administration and the citizens are always clearly defined and enacted. A vivid example of the relationship between transparency and economic development is provided by contemporary Angola. Angola is a growingly important source of oil for the developed world and its importance is enhanced by the fact that it is not an OPEC member state. The big companies extract its oil and they pay an estimated US$5 billion in revenues. However none of the companies disclose their figures. The rulers of the country and the big oil companies take full advantage of this lack of disclosure. Nobody seems to know what happens to this revenue. Angola's population is 12.4 million, of whom 82.5 per cent live in absolute or relative poverty, 62 per cent have no access to drinking water and 76 per cent have no healthcare provision.

Protective security

State institutions need to undertake measures to provide the necessary freedom to access the protection of a social security net that prevents the consequences of poverty and suffering from spreading amongst its inhabitants. Thus the state needs to provide support for the suffering caused by natural disasters, epidemics and war.

Garment factory
workers in
Narayanganj,
Bangladesh
protest against
the killing of
several workers by
police at a
demonstration
demanding the
payment of back
pay and Eid
holiday bonuses as
stipulated by
Bangladeshi
labour law.

(Fernando
Moleres/
Panos)

It should be emphasized that all these five freedoms are interconnected to each other. Each of them is of equal importance, and each has to be tackled in the development process. They are like the five equally important sides of a box in which urban investments can be contained. Success is measured by the degree to which obstructions are removed. In other words, development will inevitably get distorted if only one or two of these objectives are given a priority by using the argument that some of the freedoms can come afterwards. Although a government or collective may give priority to one freedom as the most significant pursuit, for example security of land tenure as an economic freedom, in the long run having such a narrow goal could hinder the healthy development of each citizen. Likewise it is unacceptable to have a dictatorship in order to gain quick growth in national income.

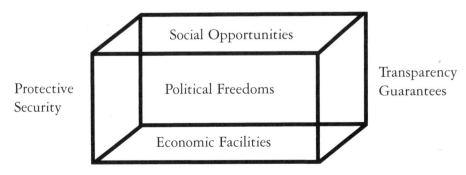

The five freedoms interconnect like five sides of a box

Prioritizing the five freedoms

A question that recurs in discussions concerning the application of Sen's Freedom Approach is the issue of prioritizing. According to Sen, if one considers prioritizing the freedoms, one takes a peculiar approach as in the process of prioritizing we would be distinguishing types rather than combinations. For example we might take economic security first and political freedom next. The question of prioritization has troubled many people. Many books have been published giving examples of the need to prioritize and the subject generates a lot of discussion. Nevertheless Sen would say it is a mistake to prioritize: 'In this regard we would be looking for the solution for just one component of freedom and not the other and that is not the way it works when considering that the relative importance we may attach to a priority might change.'

Sen reminded us how the first time the Indian electorate showed that it had any muscle at all, the government was thrown out of office not on the issue of hunger but on the issue of civil rights, namely Mrs Ghandi's suppression of fundamental rights including habeas corpus. He emphasized how the first democratic government of India lost power on account of a poor civil rights record and it has happened many times since then. Sen believes that, despite being poor, the Indian electorate was not saying that one can prioritize in such a way that political freedom does not matter until one becomes richer. On the contrary it is a question of how to interpret the circumstances:

> "priorities will take the form of the relative way we attach the different concerns of the people which become known through public discussions. It is often not recognized just how much the absence of basic civil rights affects the lives of the most deprived."

Sen recounted why one of the reasons that political and civil rights became such a big issue at the time of the emergency in India is that people were arrested, kept in prison, badly treated, beaten up and did not have an opportunity to speak with people, other poor people.

In Sen's analysis, this illustrates how in many ways civil rights are far less important for wealthier, educated people than for the slum dwellers as they were the only ones subjected to such a violent response:

> "To say that for the slum dweller what really matters is food and not civil rights is a mistake. One cannot make a priority like that. We can never get into a formula. We will have to look at the circumstance, produce the kind of appropriate analysis and then see which is the aspect we ought to emphasize now. It is a question of emphasis and the question of relative weights."

A Partial Listing of the Five Freedoms

Political freedoms

- Access to voting
- Access to law and order services
- Access to telecommunications
- Access to adequate housing
- Protection against evictions and demolitions
- Access to choose cultural/festivals/religious expressions
- Forums for free debate

Economic facilities

- For consumption, production, trade and exchange
- Access to economic resources
- Access to finance potential opportunities
- Access to explore new ways to earn livelihoods
- Access to self help solutions

Social opportunities

- Access to education, healthcare and other facilities to live a better life.
- Expression of cultural activities including daily, seasonal
- Celebrations and rituals including open spaces for festivals

Transparency guarantees

- Guarantees for openness to accurate information and disclosures.
- Evidence of trust
- Social contract between city administrators and the citizens
- Social contracts defined and enacted between the police, politicians, health
- Authorities, intelligence, developers and industry.

Protective security

- Access to protection of social security net that prevents the consequences of poverty spreading
- Natural disasters
- Epidemics
- War

- 5 -

The Need for New Evaluations

For Amartya Sen, 'The success of a society is to be evaluated primarily by the substantive freedoms that members of that society enjoy' (Sen 1999). Expansion of freedom is viewed both as the primary end and as the principal means of development. Thus one may assess the needs of development as the need to remove unfreedoms from which the members of the society may suffer. His proposition of five components or instruments of freedom are interdependent and interconnected. Indeed these interconnections are central to a fuller understanding of the instrumental role of freedom.

Existing evaluations rely on an information base that cannot provide adequate knowledge for decisive action or policies. In the urban field, this information base is dominated by the income-based poverty survey. One of the reasons for regarding this base as inadequate is that recent development literature has advocated the need for a shift towards participation and democratization through bottom-up policies. However, the view on how deprivation is measured has remained largely technocratic and top down in its evaluation. The evaluation process of measuring poverty is therefore out of synchrony with the policy goals because it does not address the potentials of individuals.

In order to redirect our development goals towards the ideal of expanding freedoms, one needs to pay closer attention to the evaluation procedures that are required to inform us of the nature of the change proposed. If one were to rely entirely on the existing evaluation methods, one would end up with inadequate data to redirect development policy goals. Existing evaluation procedures need to be supplemented with some measurement of freedom and to be better informed by a broader base in order to evaluate the potential and capability of a person who is involved in the search for a better life.

Beyond UNDP's Human Development Report

If we are to move away from the economic centred view of development towards a wider more ethical centred goal of human freedom, we need to set up a modified information base that is sensitive to freedom values rather than just economic values. Some of the pioneering work of shifting the emphasis away from development measured by economic growth toward sustainable human development values was examined by the economist Mahbub ul Haq. He was convinced that development must deal with society at large and not limit itself solely to an economic perspective. Through his enquiries, development first began to shift toward a more people-centred approach, both socially and environmentally sensitive. During his years at the UNDP (1989–95) he began work on the question of developing indicators to measure human development. The first human development report was published in 1990 and it contained evaluated data for the first time, on a global scale, that questioned the measurement of human progress through the narrow perspective of economic growth data. The data in these reports began to demonstrate the need to shift away from concerns about inequalities and move toward concerns of inhumanity. In many ways, Haq's pioneering work, which culminated at the UNDP in the annual human development reports, began a process of questioning the traditional economic notions of 'trickle down' economics. Economic growth was only the means to the real end. The real end was to continually aim for an equality of specific human development aspirations. Empowerment was to become equally relevant to the evaluations of policy goals driving successful national economies. The *Human Development Report 2000* focused on 'Human Rights and Human Development' and considerably expanded the inherent linkages between human freedom and human development. This focus has clearly emerged out of the work of Amartya Sen who wrote the first chapter of the report.

Haq highlighted the need for a better, more informative database and suggested the use of the Capability Poverty Measure (CPM) that was eventually included in the UNDP's Human Development Report 1996. This index supplemented the data derived from income poverty measurements and complemented the HDI. The CPM data considered the percentage of people who lacked minimal essential human capabilities. Three basic capabilities were measured with an overall emphasis on women:

- Nutrition and health measured the proportion of children under the age of five who were underweight.

- Safe reproduction measured the proportion of births that were unattended by health personnel.

- Education level measured the degree of female literacy.

In this evaluation, human capabilities and potentials were directly linked to deprivations experienced by women who were considered to be the centre of the family. Haq maintained that poverty could not be eradicated simply by increasing income. For a person or a family, the improvement of their condition would have to lead to an expansion of basic human capabilities leading in turn to the productive use of these capabilities. Such a contention can easily be understood if one considers the unchanged condition of a family whose income earner wastes his increased income on non- productive uses such as gambling or drinking. One of the reasons for applying non-income-based measures was to try and resolve the discussion about how much money is required to escape poverty. Income levels measured in monetary terms could only approximate ways to measure the value of goods and services. Monetary valued incomes were regarded as indicative of the purchasing power of the family or individual. But such a measure does not reflect, in all cases, the well-being of the person or his family. 'Income' is surely only a means to well-being, while enhanced 'capability' represents a closer approximation to the ends of the benefit that the individual or family seeks.

When he first put forward his ideas of evaluating capabilities, Haq did point out that the potential shortcomings of the CPM evaluation were caused by the need to rely on data collected for more traditional evaluations: 'Ideally in measuring deprivation in capabilities, indicators should be used that directly reflect capability shortfalls' (UNDP 1996). Sen discusses possible strategies to adopt to evaluate capabilities. Not all capabilities are easy to measure on metric scales so one may need to rely on supporting data from monetary-based indices. Three alternative practical approaches to overcome these difficulties and to move data collection forward are suggested:

- Direct approach – which exclusively compares data that evaluates capabilities, employment, longevity, literacy, nutrition and so on.

- Supplementary approach – which uses the traditional interpersonal income-based status evaluation and combines this with some direct approach capability data. Thus income level data could be combined with data on the availability of healthcare, evidence of gender bias in the family, extent of joblessness and so on.

- Indirect approach – which modifies the traditional income-based data through influences derived from capability data. The monetary value is therefore altered by non-monetary values. The monetary value of income is modified by the weight given by literacy levels, gender bias, unemployment and so on.

Since the goal of the wider approach to development through ever-expanding freedoms focuses on the capabilities and potentials rather than on the income of an individual, it is capability that one needs to evaluate in order to determine to what degree it is functioning or to what degree capability is obstructed.

We would therefore need to determine both the extent of unfreedoms as well as the real incomes of the citizens. In order to do this we need to modify the selection of relative weights that are used in the evaluative process. Inevitably these modified weights may not lend themselves easily to a uniformity of assessment techniques. Standard questionnaires cannot be used across different communities to evaluate their unfreedoms. Interpersonal comparisons cannot be made through standardized simple uniform question and answer procedures for data collection. The condition that is being evaluated as a constraint to freedom is, by its nature, a subjective condition. It is imperative that the current technocratic evaluations are supplemented with evaluations that have a democratic origin derived through a participatory process rather than a statistical quest. There is a need to use both qualitative and quantitative information.

Evaluating obstructions to freedom

In order to evaluate the condition of development of a community or a society, it becomes necessary to evaluate the status of the freedom of the individuals who compose the group under evaluation. In regarding these individuals as agents of change rather than patients of diagnoses or recipients of benefits, it becomes necessary to evaluate their capabilities rather than their economic condition. In other words, their deprivation is evaluated not in economic terms but in capability terms. Instead of simply evaluating income or expenditure, one needs to measure the potential of the individual and the constraints on that potential. By grouping constraints according to the five instruments of freedom, it is possible to evaluate them in terms of unfreedoms.

New indicators can provide an informational base with relative weights given to the five types of unfreedoms. Data could supply a cross measure between relative degrees of individual unfreedoms within a community as well as a basis for comparing the relative degrees of freedoms enjoyed by individuals in other communities. One could look forward to new indices being brought out reflecting the degrees of freedom enjoyed by communities – a Human Freedom Index supplemented by sub indices that could measure each of the five instruments of freedom.

Inclusive tables as well as exclusive composite indicators need to be collected and then used discriminatingly. Composite indicators can be particularly useful to assess how different policy options can affect the prospects of enhancing freedoms. Development policy will need to balance the human achievement outcomes of a policy between the different types of achievements, since all freedoms may not be accessible or realizable simultaneously. Policy makers may realize that, in the given circumstances of a case, it may be impossible to guarantee ideal political freedoms and policies would need to be devised that would distinguish between the long-term national level achievement goals and the shorter-term localized ones. Shorter-term goals could distinguish between constraints to freedom that have local origins. Such an approach would regard the overarching obstructions to freedom as an aggregate of constraints at different levels. However, such desegregating of unfreedoms does not imply any hierarchies in the components of unfreedoms; freedoms are interdependent and equally relevant. The choice of aiming at removing particular unfreedoms and not others simply enables policy makers to make realistic choices between longer-term deep-rooted constraints and others that may have local or family level impacts on the citizen. A different level of policy may be required for enabling the removal of constraints that need fundamental political and social transformations.

Ideally, the goal of a policy maker should be creating 'enabling' environments in which people's capabilities can be enhanced and their range of choices expanded. Factors preventing such enabling environments to blossom are found within all levels of society and contribute to the persistence of different unfreedoms. Effective policy making needs to be dynamic and adaptable.

Before formulating a matrix for the evaluation of freedoms, one needs to confer with the subjects of evaluation to determine their perceptions of unfreedoms. The matrix for evaluation would emerge out of public discussions so that the weights given to the indicators are understood and agreed to by the community being surveyed. Public support is a precondition for identifying criteria for evaluation.

In the following table, existing participatory and sustainability indicators are organized within Sen's five instrumental freedoms, distinguishing between those indicators that are 'technocratic', typically quantitative and exogenous, and 'participatory' indicators that are qualitative and endogenous.

Table 1: Alternative Evaluators Measuring Unfreedoms

Instruments of Freedom	Top-down, Deductive Quantitative Evaluators	Bottom-up, Inductive Qualitative Evaluators
Political freedoms	Persons imprisoned. Voting rights. Access to written, electronic, broad-cast media. Access to libraries. Women in government, police, etc. Access to telecommunication.	Constraints to voting. Access to voting booths. Constraints on legal access. Constraints on access to law and order services. Nature of land title. Constraints on access to information. Constraints to act as representatives. Constraints on use of telecommunications. Whether constitution or national law promotes the right to adequate housing. Whether constitution includes protections against eviction. Other housing-related rights (including gender sensitive). Institutional arrangements between central and local governments and balance of power between them.
Economic facilities	Male:female employment. Income. Earned income share in family. Loans from banks. Youth unemployment rate. Children in employment. Women's GDP per capita.	Percentage of family income retained by women. Loans from money lenders. Interest rate on loans compared to market rate. Individual disabilities. Constraints to mobility. Access to credit. Constraints on women to seek employment. Access to training facilities. Access to transport. Access to markets. Recovery of dues.
Social opportunities	Life expectancy. Birth and death rates. Contraception rates. Infant mortality. Maternal mortality. Infant immunization. Access to health services. Access to safe water and sanitation. Birth attended by health personal. Population per doctor. Underweight babies. Malnourished children. Calorie intake. Adult literacy. Mean years of schooling. Primary enrolment.	Access to alternative medicine practitioners. Access to fuel. Stability of dwelling. Domestic injuries. Exposure to pollution. Constraints on water access. Constraints to school attendanceVSchool drop-out rate. Unattended children. Working children under 10. Children per class. Children per teacher. Distance from primary school. Areas considered as dangerous or inaccessible to the police.
Transparency guarantees		Settlement of transacted work. Time spent on bondage obligations. Facilities to report crime. Presence of women in police station. Unreported thefts. Unreported molestation. Non formal payments for services, shelter and work. Regular independent auditing of municipal accounts. Published contracts and tenders. Sanctions against faults of civil servants. Laws on disclosure of potential conflicts of interest. Civil society involved in alteration in zoning. Civil society involved in major public projects.
Protective security	Catastrophic deaths. Destroyed houses. Destroyed schools and health centres. Epidemic cases. Density of population before and after calamity. Existence of shelters.	Access to communication networks. Access to emergency food programmes. Duration of migration. Distance of migration. Nature of resettlement. Emergency and delay. Constraints to access shelter.

- 6 -

Policy Approaches
to Underdevelopment

Experience of the UK's DFID

We can consider the approach that has been taken towards development by the UK's DFID as an example of a multi-layered approach to policy making and influencing policy. DFID is part of the IDCAs and its approach toward development has been varied for a number of reasons that relate not only to its internal changing perspectives but also to the shifting ground in the political status of the host countries where its programmes are implemented. As Michael Mutter has explained in a working paper:

"At the turn of the millennium there are mixed messages within government policies –both for national governments and for International Development Cooperation Agencies – in approaches to Urban Development and Shelter Programmes. Whilst national governments have come to understand the importance of having coherent strategies for urban development, the IDCAs have taken a different course."

The UK is such a case, the national government putting much emphasis on new thinking – for example the methodologies for regeneration and sustainable development, and more recently, the government's Urban Task Force – as much as traditional thinking that emanated from the emergence of town planning as a statutory requirement in UK from 1947 onwards (Mutter 2001).

Further endorsement of such mixed messages and variable responses to these can be seen in the two papers recently presented by Sue Unsworth, a long time employee of DFID. In these papers, she contends that donors find it easier to say 'what' needs to be done rather than 'how' it is to be done. Her analysis of the 'how' problem is extensive and far ranging.

However, it could almost be considered nebulous in the range of issues that are identified for corrective measures. The extensive range of such issues illustrates the plight of many donors who are trying to understand and then tackle underdevelopment.

Underdevelopment

In using the word 'underdevelopment' one is already calling back to past ideas and a language derived from a more classic terminology. Clearly over the past two decades, a whole host of alternative terms have superseded this in describing the conditions of poor societies, such as chronically poor, disadvantaged, economically challenged, exploited, stateless, anarchic, unstable, etc. The condition of underdevelopment has not only persisted historically across time periods, it also extends spatially across large parts of the more densely populated areas of the globe.

Understanding it has been the subject of a continuous search for generations of economists. Five decades ago it seemed that it was the economists who had a prerogative to explain theories of underdevelopment but, as the other disciplines such as sociology, political science and anthropology joined in to broaden the definition, this search for an acceptable definition of underdevelopment has become a shared pursuit. From the earlier and more simple theoretical formulations that advocated industrialization as a single point cure for underdevelopment, current development literature is multi-disciplined and advocates multi-level, multi-directional approaches.

Sue Unsworth's analysis reflects the multi-sectoral approach to tackling the wide range of symptoms that could be termed as underdevelopment. She mentions historical legacies, geography, social, economic and political processes, the role of institutions and the state as relevant to understanding the causes of poverty. Her formulations are grounded in the effort to clarify the aims and objectives of donors while assisting underdeveloped societies. In advocating what some might term a nimble-footed approach, she almost advocates an approach that relies more on the instinctive understanding of situation by the donor rather than on an evaluated one. There is a possibility that such an approach may not answer the donor's 'what and how' questions adequately.

While explaining the key themes, Unsworth has mingled the symptoms of underdevelopment with those of policy directives when the two need to be distinguished from each other simply because the ideals of the recipient seldom coincide with the more technical and bureaucratic concerns of the donor. It would be an ill-advised policy that aims at forcing the varying perceptions of the recipient and the donor to become identical as a precondition of donor policy. While focus on such key themes is undoubtedly a useful basis for a brainstorming session or a workshop to evolve strategies, it may not provide a sufficiently reliable framework for donor policy.

While the condition of underdevelopment is inherently unstable, there is a need to have a stable framework from which to view it for policy purposes. Such a policy framework needs to be both simple and also broadly acceptable to the international community in order to ensure co-operation between all the parties concerned (see (Table 3 Summary Policy Framework, page 134-135). In identifying the various issues of underdevelopment and donor responses, Unsworth may have given inadequate attention to two issues, which are important enough to need more focused attention.

First, there is the issue of the relationship between the countryside and town in underdeveloped countries. This is not only an important issue but also an unresolved one. It is one debated heatedly by donors while considering their spatial and regional priorities in locating projects and directing policy thrusts. The importance of urban centres in the midst of the crises that are unfolding in this century has been commented on above.

Second, we need to consider the important issue of inter-donor coordination. In order to tackle the wide complexities of underdevelopment through the extensive initiatives advocated by Unsworth, one would need to cast a much wider net than any unilateral aid agency could do on its own. Since it is easier to identify the problem of underdevelopment than to tackle it, one needs to consider more fully the role of international coordination in tackling it.

Unfortunately, recent events that emphasize a diminished American confidence in relying on international agencies have damaged the possibilities of effective international coordination. As George Soros has commented, those international institutions that deal with trade and global financial markets are much stronger than those that deal with social investments (Soros 2002). Issues of peace, political stability and poverty alleviation have been subjugated to issues related to trade, currencies and the movement of capital around the globe. For instance, the reluctance of the United States to pay its UN dues has undermined the role that an organization such as the UNDP could play in coordinating inter-donor efforts. Such undermining is also reinforced by EU strategies in many countries. For instance, during extensive engagements with initiating employment programmes in the Balkans, it soon became clear that, despite the fact that the programme was EU financed through the UNDP, the EU saw its identity as a contestant to the UNDP. This led to a number of futile obstacles being placed in the way of the smooth running of an obviously successful programme.

While not specially advocating the case of the UNDP, we can stress here that unilateral donor strategies often strike against the potential role of lead agencies because their own agendas are narrower than those of a lead agency. The wide policy and strategic aims advocated by Unsworth cannot be successfully implemented without lead agencies. Such a lead agency could hold up the framework through which donors could address their individual concerns in each country. Inevitably each donor has a unique relationship with the recipient country that is based on special historic links as well as their own metropolitan compulsions. These unilateral concerns need to be addressed in each donor programme. However, if one were to define a simple framework at the lead agent's level, then donors could enter the field through this common framework and submit the results of their initiatives to a common evaluation procedure, thus formulating a shared platform for the evaluation of successes and failures.

Urban livelihoods

Lloyd-Jones and Rakodi's *Urban Livelihoods* gives an account of the multi-dimensional approach to development taken by DFID (Lloyd-Jones and Rakodi 2002). This book defines more extensively the compendium of analyses, policies and programmes used by DFID. A wide range of approaches has been assembled in an effort to address the multiple dimensions of poverty alleviation. This omnibus approach casts a wide net and catches almost all the problematic symptoms of the poverty of underdevelopment. Any predefined policy framework for such an approach would inevitably be very complex. The emphasis and priority of the overarching goal of sustainability and poverty reduction is clear. Indeed so is the emphasis on a people-centred approach clearly articulated:

> *"Inherent in this conception of livelihoods is the notion that the relative poverty or economic well being of poor people should be understood from the point of view of the people themselves. This people-centred view provides a balance to the global and more strategic perspective normally offered by a sustainable development policy approach."*

The approach advocated in the book regards the individual as the possessor of livelihood assets, as a producer of wealth. Development initiatives are seen as enhancers of these assets, so the level of livelihood assets can be enhanced by effective development policies. These assets are composed of five capitals, and policies are required to enhance the value of these capitals. In adopting this approach, emphasis is placed on reversing the 'deprived' condition of the recipient and substituting it with a description of him as an asset-owning member of a community. The assets of the poor are to be protected form vulnerabilities.

These assets are listed as follows (no particular sequence):

- Financial – savings, access to credit.

- Human – labour, health, education, other skills.

- Natural – urban agriculture, rivers, land.

- Physical – housing, livestock, economic and social infrastructure, production equipment.

- Social – social support mechanisms, information.

The vulnerabilities of the poor are listed as follows:

- Legal status – informal wage employment, shelter, land, political rights.

- Services and infrastructure – lack of basic social services.

- Local environment – poor physical environment, socially challenged environments.

- Dependence on the cash economy – vulnerability to fluctuating market prices.

From the above analysis, it can be seen that the DFID approach to development and the approach advocated by Sen are mutually interlinked. However the merit of the framework being proposed focuses on the concept of freedom to replace the overarching goal of poverty removal policies with the more desirable goal of expanding individual freedoms to enable a person to live the life that he values. While the DFID approach regards the productive status of the individual, the Freedom Approach emphasizes his potential to be free. DFID's goal of removing poverty is contrasted with the Freedom Approach goal of enhancing freedom. Poverty eradication and increase in income are the means, while the pursuit of freedoms are the ends that reach out to the broader ideal of the human beings.

"I would argue that the Sustainable Livelihood's approach draws less direct links between agency and structure. That is because it has a less focus than Sen on politics and political institutions. For Sen the overall achievement of development as freedom is deeply contingent on political and social arrangements and the way they come together. There is a big difference between seeing institutions as intervening

*variables, as happens in the sustainability and liveli-
hood approach, and seeing democracy and public
action as a development needs event. While both
approaches look at individual agency, the
Sustainable Livelihoods approach doesn't disaggre-
gate the challenges and contributions of the poor on
the basis of gender. It doesn't look at particular
issues facing the men and women and the relationships between them in building up their asset base. It
doesn't articulate a gender perspective and for Sen
that is a very crucial part of Development as Freedom,
a recognition of women's role – as one that warrants
noting that some variables relate directly to women's
agency and structural position."*

Jo Beall, LSE Colloquium, 7 July 2003

Rights approach

Like Sen's Freedom Approach, the rights-based approach also places the
individual at the centre of its concerns. Each individual has inalienable
human rights that spring from the 1948 UN Declaration and other
covenants which define these as being born free and equal in dignity and
rights. Broadly speaking, these rights also cover, as does the Freedoms
spectrum, economic, social, cultural and political aspects. The differences
between the two approaches relate to the interpretation of the causes of
poverty and the strategy required for a solution. The rights-based
approach assumes that there is a hidden bag containing fundamental
rights – perhaps God given – that have to be taken or claimed from the
authorities or those in power. It also assumes that these powers have the
legitimacy to give these rights. Rights have to be wrested from exploitative authorities and the declarations and covenants are very much a part of
a declaratory strategy which calls for the implementation of international
institutional resolutions regardless of the cultural or social endowments of
the claimants.

The freedoms approach, on the other hand, is not declaratory and does
not assume that freedom has to be regained. The Freedom Approach
enables the individual to lead the life they value leading and that may
include choices realized through a changing awareness arising from new
information or a series of circumstances and values. The social choices
become known and recognized through the process of enabling one's own
potential and capability through the freedom to engage in participation
and public discussions. Presently DFID is committed to a rights-based

approach in order to reduce poverty outcomes, as measured by the Millennium Development Goals (MDGs). DFID's Target Strategy Paper on Participatory Rights Assessment Methodologies (PRAMS) identifies three main principles:

- Participation: from passive beneficiaries to active and empowered citizens.

- Inclusion: all human rights for all people.

- Fulfilling obligation: to protect, promote and ensure the realization of all human rights.

The development of freedoms is more fundamental than the PRAMS approach in its starting position to review the mechanism of social choice theory and social agency. The sole principle is removing obstructions to the free agency of the individual without placing any single unfreedom as a priority. Each freedom consists of rights and opportunities and each of them needs to be gained 'to advance the capability of a person'.

Obstructions to freedoms and free agency are not held in a bunch by anybody in particular, as the value added will change with each situation, community and individual. Each of the freedoms is interlinked and present in every situation and their co-partnership results in strengthening each aspect beyond their independent strengths. Giving freedom of economic facilities and prosperity may lead to better access to social opportunities and health. Health can be identified by a series of characteristics including nutrition, a women's appreciation of her self within the obligations of family responsibilities, access to medical experts, as in the case of attitudes in Islamic communities (like Afghanistan) to male doctors treating women. The granting of all human rights does not automatically lead to achievements in all social, economic, political and cultural domains as the obstructions to free individual agency could still persist in open democratic societies.

UN-HABITAT Agenda

There is, in the international arena, an approach towards urban development that largely coincides with the Freedom Approach. Localizing the Habitat Agenda uses an internationally agreed policy framework to address the issues of poverty. UN-member states signed this Agenda in Istanbul in 1996.[9] It is recognized as a common urban agenda for the twenty-first century and introduced 'Urbanization and Sustainable Urban Development' as a theme to evaluate the continuing deterioration in shelter and human settlements.

The Habitat Agenda recognizes that the issue of rapid urbanization and the growing number of poor people concentrated in cities has become a

Sustainable human settlements

Making towns, cities and villages more sustainable through integrated planning and management, as well as the appropriate regulation of services and the environment.

Financing shelter and human settlements

Mobilizing more money for local economic development through new and innovative approaches such as public-private partnership.

Good urban governance

Enablement and participation: urban development through involvement of people in decision making, action and partnership.

The Habitat Agenda

Istanbul declaration of goals and principles

Gender equality

Taking account of the needs of women and men in decision making at every level.

Assessing progress

Developing the systems and indicators to monitor progress.

Adequate shelter for all

Access to land, with security of tenure equal property rights for women and access to essential services.

International cooperation

Improving coordination, exchange of information and best practice between nations.

Source: DFID (2001), *Meeting the Challenge of Poverty in Urban Areas.*

The seven Habitat Agenda commitments

major concern for governments and communities in developing countries. The Agenda has been used as a common ground and a shared vehicle for formulating policies and practices. It could provide a key tool for the narrower goals of urban poverty reduction through local development initiatives, using best practice approaches, by working with national governments.

The Agenda commitments are based on the upholding of human rights and enabling the poor to participate in decision making and to benefit from development process. However, the localizing process of the Agenda has some limitations, as it does not entirely address urban poverty adequately.

Apart from the fact that the Agenda is only advisory, there is not enough coordination, understanding, involvement and obligation from all sectors to address the Agenda commitments effectively (Max Lock Centre and WEDC 2002). This experience helps one to understand the inherent problems of having a common policy framework that may be too narrow in its perspective to make it coincide with all the participants' individual goals. In some sense it would help to define the common framework to focus on a broader development goal such as the one advocated by Sen that centres on unfreedom rather than on poverty. In some countries – for example, Spain and to a certain extent Brazil– there are good examples of successful implementation as a result of effective networking from various agencies. This suggests there should be ways and means to strengthen the role of UN-HABITAT, establish networking, improve and reform the broader goal of development and promote the use of a more effective best practice approach for policy and programme implementation. Essentially it endorses the need for a lead agency to coordinate donor policies (DFID 2001).

The International Urban Development Goals of the Habitat Agenda are further backed by the Millennium Development Goals (UN, 2000). Target 11 sets out clearly the goal of improving the lives of at least 100 million slum dwellers by 2020. The Habitat Agenda has all the ingredients for orchestrating a concerted and coordinated effort to foster development in urban areas. It highlights the potential role of networking among all levels of stakeholders in urban development and focuses on the promising action by the 'Habitat Agenda Partners' – the full range of participants from all levels from international agencies to local communities – including NGOs, the private sector and all levels of government. They all play essential roles in strengthening the commitment to achieve the Urban Development Goals set out in the Habitat Agenda while suggesting the formation of global, national and local action networks to achieve the commitments.

As one of the Habitat Agenda partners and an international donor agency, DFID recognizes the goals and targets set by the United Nations and especially Habitat Agenda and has supported the implementation of the Habitat Agenda localization approaches and the application of a best practice policy framework. This is part of a global strategy set out in the DFID plan Meeting the Challenge of Poverty in Urban Areas (DFID 2001). This continues the recognition of the need to deal with urban poverty as was laid out in the 1997 UK Government White Paper on international development. The plan outlines 5 key actions:

- Enable the poor to participate in the decision-making process, and to benefit from urban development.

- Develop the capacity of local actors to manage pro-poor urban development and regional growth.

- Support national governments to strengthen the legislative and regulatory framework within which city-based development takes place.

- Strengthen efforts by the international community to support the urbanization process, which involves the participation of poor people.

- Improve DFID's and others capacities to address the urban challenge through information support and knowledge and research development.

Some countries that have signed The Habitat Agenda have formed Habitat Committees to follow up on their commitment. Limited success has been achieved in localizing the Habitat Agenda, for example in Spain's use of a best practice approach. Stronger networking at all government levels of each country is needed to make sure that the Habitat Agenda development goals are understood and implemented. Finding out and strengthening appropriate means of mediation within the various governance and institutional arrangements in the whole networking process appears to be an essential element. At present, there is little evidence of any conscious use of Habitat Agenda by local communities. The UN-HABITAT Best Practice Database has few examples of good practices by local communities in support of urban poverty reduction. This may reflect the fact that there is not enough capacity for local communities to use a best practice approach, especially among the urban poor. Unfortunately only some NGOs and organizations in the education sectors and very few in the private sectors are committed to the implementation of Habitat Agenda. However, with increasing understanding of these issues, there are undoubtedly growing numbers of actors who have started focusing on achieving the development goals of the Habitat Agenda. These actors do not stand independently but interrelate to each other in their development approach. These links are important and need to be reinforced.

Existing international urban development approaches do need a simpler framework to relate their co-ordinated efforts. While earlier efforts had focused entirely on physical and infrastructure development strategies the need to address the wider social economic and political aspects of development is being recognized by policy makers. Such a strategy requires higher levels of participatory activities from the community.

While community participation has now been recognized and implemented in many urban development policies of international agencies as well as other actors in local government, civic society and NGOs, the need for a common framework through which all these coordinated efforts are interlinked is required. While it focuses on human settlements and housing,

Table 2: A Comparison of Goals

Existing strategies and policy goals compared to the development as five freedoms approach.

Development as Freedom	Habitat Agenda	DFID urban strategy 2002
Political freedom	Decentralization and strengthening of local authorities, association and networks. Popular participation and civic engagement. Participatory and consultative mechanisms. Capacity building and institutional development.	Develop the capacity of local actors to manage pro-poor urban development and regional growth. Strengthen efforts by the international community to support the urbanization process which involves the participation of poor people. Need for governments to provide the right enabling, legislative and regulatory framework, pro-poor and market sensitive. Empowering poor people themselves to demand and realize their rights and entitlements. Optimize the opportunities offered by decentralization. Support to civil society groups to advocate poor people's needs and to participate in political systems.
Economic facilities	Financing shelter and human settlements. Gender equality. Improving urban economies. Enabling markets to work. Mobilizing finance sources. Ensuring access to land.	Support to the private sector for PPP, business and socially responsible business. DFID will work to increase the capacity of cities to attract investment and to develop improved links with rural economies. Need to ensure that the distribution of the opportunities of economic growth reach the poor. Develop the capacity of local actors to manage pro-poor urban development and regional growth.
Social opportunities	Need for economic development, social development and environmental protection. Ensuring access to basic infrastructure. Environment sustainability. Conservation of historic and cultural heritage.	DFID will contribute to programmes that help to improve the living and working conditions of the poor: water and sanitation; energy sources; tenure arrangements; supply of land for housing and health and safety. Poor people should benefit from improved healthcare, better education opportunities.
Transparency guarantees	Strengthen shelter related information system.	Improve DFID's and others capacities to address the urban challenge through information support, and knowledge and research development. Improve local accountability systems. Need to access and to share information so to negotiate on a more equal footing with others.
Protective security	Disaster prevention, mitigation and post-disaster rehabilitation capabilities.	

Habitat Agenda is not wide enough in its scope to cover the instruments that are defined by Sen. However, some of the issues are partially embedded into the different sets of headings of the context of human settlements. The Habitat Agenda is more specific in its emphasis on community urban poverty, especially in respect of housing and achieving sustainable urban development. The Agenda goals do however emphasize the need to uphold human rights and enable the poor to participate in decision making and to benefit from the development process. The right to development offers a means to greater stability and peace in the world. Democracy enables such development through human rights, transparent representation, an accountable government and administration and effective participation. It also recognizes the right to development of various religious and ethical values, cultural backgrounds and philosophical convictions.

In Table 2 we have listed policies as they were at the time of research as this exercise is valid as an example of how any institution, agency or government department can re-evaluate their policy objectives within the five-freedom framework.

Freedom, democracy and participatory action

Where the basic needs perspective went wrong, according to Sen, was to treat human beings as patients rather than agents of change. It assumed people do not have the choice to make decisions regarding the kind of life they want to lead. Humans being are agents of change. In this respect earlier urban development polices, according to Sen, have been responsible for creating situations:

> *"in which these robust thoughts that we need for living as fulfilled human beings are lost. If you have to decide what has to be done in the slums it is not a question of what the slum dwellers need – you have to find out what they could do if they had the freedom to do it."*
> 10

The impact of how you decide to enhance the freedom will be influenced by the kind of criteria and information base you have.

In Sen's opinion, our ideas of needs is based on the condition of what we are, which in most cases might appear to be like a small cog in a large wheel. He illustrates a current scenario in society where traffic in our modern cities has grown out of control. We need some sort of transport, for example a bicycle or a car, to get from one place to anther. We may be aware that the increase in cars has a direct effect on the quality of life in the city including pollution, noise, and traffic. The question is how can we begin to think about reorganizing this society in regard to the priority and needs of transportation? For that, Sen advised that you need to have some sort of participatory process to establish a need alteration – which may determine the need to increase the incentive to have bicycles and public transport. What we call needs are, according to Sen, not just things we want, but conditional on the nature of the society and generated by society. Needs are thoroughly contingent on knowledge and acquiring knowledge is based on communication, based on schools and media discussion. We see and experience these needs as concerns we can do something about. Nonetheless he explained that to get to this stage of needs and need alteration you need the freedom, the political freedom to discuss and participate in making the solutions that will reflect the values of the people.

In his first book, *Choice of Techniques*, Sen explained he was trying to get the attention of development to shift away from income and wage inequality to needs. Increasingly he felt that he was really barking up the wrong tree in giving needs a profundity that it did not have because fundamentally human beings are people who are agents of change.

> "The agent view of life includes the freedom to not only question what we can do with our lives but also what we want to do – what kind of needs would we generate in the type of society we would like to live in."

A concern raised by David Satterthwaite during the discussions at LSE Colloquium highlighted how Sen's Freedom Approach provides only a framework, but no political means to realize the freedom. A prime example is in India. Even though there has been a democracy for 50 years the city of Mumbai is still home to 5.5 million slum dwellers. The National Slum Dwellers Federation (NDSF) in Mumbai represents these people who have almost no income and no official address. Satterthwaite explained that without an official address it is impossible to acquire a ration card and, because these people live on land to which someone else claims ownership, the slum dwellers have no right to occupy. They have no toilets and must negotiate with some other community to use their toilet or defecate out in the open. The success of the NSDF has shown the only chance of achieving individual freedom is through organization, demonstration and then bringing the state into negotiation. Local organization and local action create the political means to deliver freedoms.

In response, Sen said he believed there was a slight danger in assuming a correlation between the continued existence of slum dwellers in India and India as a working democracy. One reality does not dismiss the other. The lives of the slum dwellers must be addressed 'and that will depend on democracy which is public reasoning—that's the way to understand it.' The process is not like that of Samuel Hunting who said; 'that nothing else is there other than just election, fair and free election,' implying the rest of individual and collective participation processes are not a matter of democracy. That is not the way that democracy has taken place in the past. We must not overlook the long tradition of public reasoning in different parts of the world. Participation at the local, national and various intermediate levels is part of the democratic life one is seeking.[11]

Sen explained that in his opinion the work of SPARC and NSDF, local organization and local action does deliver freedoms. This forms part of the analysis.

> *"If you are concerned with the lives of the people you will emphasize the importance of every consideration and action that will effect those lives. If local action emerges as being the right objective of the project then you focus on this activity. There is no tension between the Freedom Approach and local action, on the contrary, SPARC has supported the process of local organization and action for the NSDF and through these activities they have achieved freedoms that would not have happened otherwise. For that reason you evaluate the achievements in the lives of the individuals in question through the collective action."[12]*

During the same debate, Lord Meghnad Desai emphasized that one does not achieve democracy and freedom and stop. In his opinion there is not a stop option. Yet exclusions exist and one has to think imaginatively about how to overcome them in that respect. In his opinion, a lot of freedoms were won by collective actions which were often opposed by other collectivities. For example he cited the suffragette movement in the United Kingdom that involved a minority group of women and became one of the most noted violent movements, and was opposed root and branch by the political leaders at that time. In this instance Desai reminded us how the Prime Minister believed the majority of his voters were against women's rights. He was a democrat and questioned why the suffragettes were pressuring an undemocratic solution on him. In Desai's opinion, of course it was not an undemocratic solution because as seen in this example the collective action by a portion of the people can advance freedoms. Desai emphasized: 'one must never forget, a lot of the freedoms achieved by the trade union movement and by the women's movement were often under extreme protest. One must not fall into the trap of believing that parliamentary methods alone can be used'. There is no limit as to how much more can be achieved because in his opinion: 'I don't see any democracy as actually being more than a reasonably imperfect democracy.'

National and international action

Global policy makers question how to introduce the Freedom Approach to countries that are not interested whether they are democracies or non-democratic governments. According to Sen, the Freedom Approach should be discussed, adopted and reappraised, particularly in recognized democratic society, in order to evaluate the obstructions to participation and social decision making. It is equally valid in a non-democratic country which may not value participation processes at all. He explained that one might find it difficult to establish a dialogue with a government or with policy makers of countries that are not interested. Sen reminded us that not every government or policy maker thinks of adopting a people-centred approach that will enable human development aspirations to be achieved. The numbers of non-democratic governments that exist would exclude 40 per cent of the world from considering a Freedom Approach today. One might assume these non-democratic governments are therefore excluded from even considering the Freedom Approach in the sense that you might not to want to work for them. Sen agreed that, indeed, one might have every reason not to want to work for them. He certainly would not advise a government that had no concern for democratic objectives. On the other hand he believed this fact alone does not detract from considering whether these ideas would be of benefit. In Sen's opinion it would not be contradictory to use these ideas in undemocratic governments. On the contrary he advised, "one hopes it undermines their thinking to some extent".

There is always the possibility that the Freedom Approach may be interpreted very differently. Sen suggested we look back at Stalin's Russia with its gulags, etc. In the history of world, Russia expanded the concept of giving basic education to all of Soviet Asia even further than the empire had achieved. He explained how it was an imperial power, but it was a different imperial power from the British Empire and varied sharply in regard to attitudes to education in what were affectively conquered and subjugated territories. Consequently, he concluded, when discussing what can be made of the Freedom Approach, in the context of changing the lives of human beings, we will have to marry our reading of which government will do what and whether by and large it deserves your help or it does not. 'That is the kind of questions that we cannot escape.'

In Sen's view, it is clear that development approaches can be manipulated to coerce and influence communities for private or ideologically economic goals. "This is exactly what dictators do. This is part of our intellectual territory, and has to be distinguished from considering whom it is that we, as responsible human beings, would like to help." Sen explained that this is an individual question and he has never advised any government in his life and not because every government imposed dreadful policies in regard to human development goals; rather he has been lucky living in democratic countries in India, Europe and America. In fact Sen described how he presents his ideas to any public domain and in this respect it depends on whether the UN or government X or government Y or the World Bank decides to take them up.

Part III

Formulating Policy Frameworks

"It is a question of deciding on how to plan for the city. By that I mean the unfreedoms of the city being balanced against the freedom of the human being living in society to choose the kind of world they want in which the mega-cities are up for contention. We have to see that we have much more freedom to arrange atmospheres in which the unfreedoms can be avoided. That to me is the central challenge."

Amartya Sen, Cambridge, 2002

- 7 -

The Challenge

The difficulties of adopting shared policy frameworks and trying to implement them across a variety of communities are not easy to overcome. Even if the wider goals of freedom were to be adopted by all, the kinds of difficulties faced on the ground by agencies would surely continue. For instance, the commitment by the United Nations, through UN-HABITAT, is clearly apparent in its support for participation in the Habitat Agenda. However, at the ground level there are difficulties. The Agenda is poorly followed up in many countries due to the limitations of local governments who do not understand the scope of work, or due to the nature of political representation and local political priorities. It is not easily to pursue the Agenda commitment down to the lowest local level. Even though the nature of participation is recognized by various international development agencies, and despite the promotion of a 'bottom-up' approach, there are severe implementation problems on the ground. It is possible that this complex process requires a longer period of time to monitor the results than may be considered realistic by all international agencies, due to their administrative and political constraints.

While national governments need to be at the forefront of this implementation, in most cases, especially in developing countries, there is lack of technical, financial and human capacity, as well as political will, to manage this process. Other actors such as NGOs, the private sector and education institutions have a very limited role, even though some of them have successfully supported the participation process. The community needs to be assisted directly through a fuller participation process. Using the participatory process in collecting evaluation data could enable this to happen. Such participatory evaluation will need to determine whether local communities have enough freedom of opportunity to participate and whether the community will share this freedom with the actors who are promoting development. Such issues will need to be evaluated at all levels of work:

International

At an international level, development agendas are often initiated and then implemented through national level institutions. Such national level institutions do not necessarily represent community interests. There is a need to make local communities more aware of this complex situation and use their voice to participate in the development process. One example of good practice in this area is illustrated by the participation of the National Slum Dwellers Federations who attended the World Urban Forum.

National

At a national level, national governments are often viewed as sole mediators by the international agencies. There is a need for the national agency to allow local communities to organize themselves and for them to relax strict centralized regulations and limitations on local initiatives in urban development. There may be a need to take steps to allow local urban governance to emerge as a more representative form of urban community freedom. However, any local, community-empowered government may not have sufficient power and capacity to deliver development goals. In this case, their capacities to govern at each level would need to be strengthened in an appropriate way so that the freedoms sought by the development process can be adequately supported.

Private

At the private mediator level, most NGOs that are funded by international agencies try to bring international agency development goals to local communities. This needs to allow the full participation of communities in the consolidation of the goals that they value.

Local

At a local community level, poor communities and their representative organizations in urban areas often lack technical capacity. They have potentials and capabilities that are often not recognized by any agencies working in the area. In using freedom as the goal of development, it is these potentials and capabilities that will be of prime importance as the focus of any development programme situated in the community.

Some of the wider concerns for a policy framework need to address the deeper constraints on development. These constraints could have cultural or historical facets which impinge on rights and capabilities of people due to ethnic, social or other causes. Amartya Sen explains: "One view sees development as a 'fierce' process, with much 'blood, sweat and tears' – a world in which wisdom demands toughness" (Sen 1999). There is no place for 'luxurious' ideas of democracy, or for political and civil rights. In this view, policy makers are convinced that they know best what is needed at the macro level and the immediate sacrifice of the population in terms of hardship and lack of freedom is seen as a small price to pay for later benefits. This has parallels with the World Bank and IMF's justification for the possible short-term hardship endured by the poor following the imposition of Structural Adjustment Programmes. The other alternative view "sees development as essentially a 'friendly' process." One in which people participate and are included and have a voice in determining the direction of development and its priorities as well as in the identification of constraints. Those formulating policy frameworks will inevitably need to be informed of which of these views is being adopted both for long term as well as short term strategies.

A simpler framework would enable communication between sponsors to be carried out in a coordinated manner. It would provide them with a common sounding board for their evaluations.

Instead of each sponsor holding up unique multi-directional programmes and policies as an end, it could be possible to place these varied policies within a simple development framework that would enable cooperation between sponsors.

The role of the evaluator

The measurement of poverty is influenced, not only by the outlook but also by the goals of the evaluator. If a policy relies on a top-down approach it will exclude the poor from the process of both drafting and implementation policies and may thereby reflect the dominance of income-based indicators. In an urban setting, these indicators have been shown to systematically underestimate the scale of poverty. Satterthwaite and Jonsson concluded that the income-based poverty indicator: "has no validity unless it accurately reflects the income level that an individual or household needs to avoid 'poverty in their particular neighbourhood (whether it is a village, small town, city or large metropolis)", (Satterthwaite and Jonsson 2001).

As local and national governments struggle to cope with the rate of urban growth, they look toward 'orthodox' development packages based on heavy infrastructure investments as a way out of the anarchy that threatens to engulf them as migration to the urban areas continues. But this reliance on infrastructure investments needs to be balanced with initiatives to remove constraints on local governance, citizenry and individual agency. People have to get together and rely on themselves to make up for the defects of their policy makers and implementers, and the lack of funding. Much literature on community organization or on the growth of the informal sector has been published, but development agencies and policy makers do need to keep themselves informed of the complexity and dynamics of the new megalopolis. Undoubtedly policies have been slowly moving away from a top-down model of development. Nevertheless, there is a need to craft adequate tools to measure the constraints on urban development as seen in the light of the need to remove unfreedoms. The 'inclusive city' needs to be measured in a new light, with the individual as the main agent of development at the centre.

The analysis of the status of development in any society requires evaluation that is grounded on some sort of informational base. There is a need to identify the characteristics that are seen to be relevant in evaluating the development potential of a society and to measure them as indicators. A wide range of indicators can be used to compose the information base. There is no unique and exclusive way to compose it. Currently perhaps the most complex exercise for evaluating development on a common index is that used by UNDP for their Human Development Report (HDR).

New evaluations at the UNDP

Human development as a concept is larger than its measurement. At present the HDI only measures concrete capabilities of living a healthy life, through determining the time span of a long life and through life expectancy at birth and childhood mortality rates. Included in this measurement is the capability to access knowledge through literacy and education. These measures are all indicators that can be linked as assets to the income capability characteristics of current development goal policy. However HDI does not measure the freedom of social choice as the mechanism necessary to determine the value of living a healthy life or well-being as a goal in itself.

According to Antonio Vigilante, UNDP Resident Coordinator for operational activities in Egypt, the HDR originally saw the light as a global instrument but has now been nationalized and even localized..

In Egypt, for instance, UNDP is preparing one human development report for each one of the 27 regions of the country, so bringing the analysis of human development, including the calculation of the Human Development Index, down to the level of municipalities and the level of villages. In such a way, it is possible to know a wealth of information that is critical to understand human development gaps and geographic disparities and the different needs and demands that vary from one region of the country to the other.

Along with localizing the HDI, UNDP are taking a different look at poverty measurement. Normally this is calculated according to expert points of view and statistical data. 'Objective' poverty lines are thus obtained. But no matter how sophisticated these methodologies are, and some of them have become indeed quite sophisticated by now, they still represent an abstract construct. Therefore UNDP have also conducted 'subjective' poverty line studies recently, which consist in asking the people themselves to define what is poverty and what is not, if they are below or up the poverty line. The results of such surveys are very interesting because, when compared with 'objective' poverty line measurement, they may show significant differences.

In Egypt objective poverty incidence is found to be highest in the rural areas and in the south of the country. Subjective poverty is found highest in the north of the country and in urban areas. This is understandable, since poverty is, in its essence, a relative concept and condition. This relativity of poverty perceptions predominates when asking people to assess themselves in their situation. The comparison with the neighbours and with their environment influences decisively their perception and self-assessment of being poor or not poor.

These different perceptions cannot be ignored. By putting all this wealth of data and analysis out in the public domain should spark a dialogue on different approaches that will identify development constraints and surface previously ignored hard political choices and trade-offs. UNDP have used new instruments in several towns to survey and identify people's aspirations. Although the country contexts can be very different and relatively more or less sophisticated, the instrument of human representative surveys can be used in different forms. For example human security surveys, to understand whether people feel vulnerable, aspirations surveys, to see what really people wish and youth aspirations surveys. There are a whole array of similar instruments, from using the media through 'call in' programmes to printed press surveys and questionnaires. Consequently these tools can help gain a better understanding as to whether development cooperation operators and the government policy makers respond well to people's aspirations. If not these tools can consequently identify possible gaps in understanding and diagnosis. Too often policy makers and development operators double guess, 'interpret', assume people's needs, without verification and validation by the people themselves.

All these instruments are only analytical tools and information that need to be 'operationalized' and completed within participatory approaches in programme design, monitoring and evaluation. For example a few years ago the UNDP helped prepare and implement a programme for the lowland indigenous people of Bolivia. Through the interpretation and analytical support of community leaders and anthropologists, they worked directly with 29 indigenous groups to help them define their own priorities. The results of such participative process revealed a difference from what we may have thought. Starting with a self census, (a census conducted by the same indigenous groups) even the very statistical information would have been collected, owned and prepared by the people intended to be supported by the UNDP.

One of the surprising findings of the participative needs assessment was that the indigenous groups' priority was radio communications. Had the UNDP proceeded in a more conventional programme formulation mode, they would have probably said that education or health services provision would have been their priority. Instead the barrier the indigenous groups wanted to break first was isolation. UNDP might never have assigned such high priority to this. Consequently development as freedom for them was the choice to establish more and better communications than basic services. Such a decentralized participatory approach to project formulation is not only fair but also increases development assistance effectiveness and efficiency.

In Egypt, after having calculated the Human Development Index, at local level and at municipal level, UNDP have selected the 60 bottom municipalities and are validating the data with citizen's participation. By holding all kinds of stakeholders meetings, UNDP aim to find out whether the data is telling the true story or whether there are hidden local development constraints that people identify, beyond all statistical analysis. On the basis of that, UNDP will build up, for each one of the municipalities, a local recovery programme, funded by government and donors.

The challenge of finding instruments (in the formulation, monitoring and evaluation of programmes) that will ensure more accountability to the communities is not yet fully addressed. It is important to try even more to make people the owners of development projects and ensure those programmes interpret their ambitions well and encourage them to evaluate the impact. Presently there is nothing that measures freedom or the absence of corruption and the protection of individual social agency in the human security point of view. The Freedom Approach is a complement that would make the indicator capable of better measuring human development than it does right now. Removing Unfreedoms would be seen as filling in a gap in the human development approach already working.

Antonio Vigilante, LSE Colloquium (DFID 2003)

Choice of indicators

The choice of the information base as well as the particular indicators that are measured influences the resultant policy. But, as Sen has pointed out in his book (1999), 'There is no royal road to evaluation of economic and social policies'. In order to maximize the usefulness of evaluative techniques, one needs to reflect on the variety of considerations that influence each individual in the community. Existing development policies are inevitably multi-layered. This is partially due to the multiple institutions that are involved in sponsoring development. There are national governments, international agencies and a host of multi-lateral arrangements that influence development policies. National governments sponsor development initiatives through a wide range of accelerators such as neighbourhood organizations; community-based institutions, NGOs and municipalities as well as national bodies. International institutions direct their initiatives through NGOs, UN agencies, as well as national governments' IDCAs. A multi-layered approach thus provides flexibility that can be inclusive of the special interests of these sponsors. To a certain extent, this approach provides a flexibility that could be considered as being more responsive.

The need for a shared policy framework

There is a need to provide a simpler framework within which these multi-layered approaches can operate. Such a simple framework would enable evaluation and feedback to be a shared process. A simpler framework would enable communication between sponsors to be carried out in a coordinated manner. It would provide them with a common sounding board for their evaluations. Instead of each sponsor holding up unique multi-directional programmes and policies as an end, it could be possible to place these varied policies within a simple development framework that would enable cooperation between the sponsors to a much higher order than has hitherto been possible. This framework would in no way constrain the different sponsors from selecting their own individual or cooperative programmes and policies; it would simply enable all of them to understand each other's approach in relation to a common development framework. A simple common development framework should founded on the higher goals of improving the human condition by defining an ultimate goal of development strategies as one that provides ever-expanding freedoms to the citizens of each country. (See Table 3 for Summary Policy Framework, pages 134-135).

- 8 -

Universal and Varying Values

Policy makers may wonder whether evaluations of Sen's Freedom Approach can be taken as something valid, tested and applicable at a micro, individual level and at the macro country level. Can it go so far as to initiate policy discussion that can reorder the priorities of the country – not only in terms of process but also in terms of objectives? According to Sen there are those in development work who might identify the diversity of freedoms desired by individuals within a community but yet be unclear as how to formulate an urban initiative. For example many individuals will live in a society and be attached to many different types of freedoms. There may be a conflict between the freedoms it is possible to achieve for all these various individuals. The freedoms required by each individual are representative of what are called varying values, values that vary according to the view of those who hold them as important to their well-being.

For example, varying values often reflect the diversity of cultural expression, so at this level the freedoms are very specific. At other levels, Sen explained, the freedoms are very general, for example, the need for shelter. Universally human beings need to be sheltered for reasons of privacy and for protection from the elements, to have comfortable night's sleep, and for a whole host of other reasons. One could say that shelter is a universal need. Yet Sen questioned what kind of shelter it might be?

> "Would it be a Japanese-style building, or a western type bungalow? Or the kind of building that in Bangladesh the community might feel is a priority. Internationally the demand for Bangladesh-type accommodation might be quite small. And, if we were to evaluate the need for a Bangladesh-type shelter in Texas we would find there might be no demand at all. It would be a mistake to say these needs are not universal because underlying the expression of shelter we are considering the need to be sheltered. It is the characteristic we are looking at."

In order to clarify a greater understanding in this discussion, Sen referred to economic literature, and the economists Michael Peacock and

Claire Gorman at London School of Economics who discussed 'characteristics' in their work. The feature of characteristics can be understood when viewing the variety of biscuits or types of bread. In the end what you are looking for is nutrition, that is the characteristic. In a sense the commodities that are characteristic (nutrition in this case) are the feature.

> *"Our evaluation of particular needs, like a need for a Bangladesh bungalow compared with need for shelter, has a common feature shared between them – protection from the elements in order to survive. They are universal in the sense that they are valued for much the same reason. Obviously the extent to which you need a shelter will depend on what kind of planet you live on and on the characteristics around you. Whether you are an Eskimo or Congolese, you will need a denser building if you happen to be in a colder climate than you would if you happen to be in a warmer climate. That does not make it arbitrary and culturally dependent. When one makes a claim about universality, it is in the context of it being contingent on needs given the circumstances and at a general level."*

Amartya Sen, LSE Colloquium

Re-ordering priorities

It would be easy to assume that there could be a conflict in addressing the priorities of different types of needs, for example, shelter, food or education if there is a limited amount of income. According to Sen, it is scarcity that makes us choose between these needs. "It is a sensitive issue that if you are poor then you may have to choose between having basic shelter or having better food. Then the question arises, what are the priorities of these choices?"

According to Sen, in resolving this question of re-ordering priorities in different circumstances, you participste in a long standing historical philosophical discussion. He referred to Aristotle, who, as you may expect, set out a clear ranking linear progression whereby the life of the intellectual is the highest need. "There is something grand about it" as Sen explained, "because like Adam Smith, Aristotle also thought every human being is capable of intellectual activity in some way." However there will be others who may disagree and take a narrower interpretation, a sectarian, racist view and argue that not every human being has the potential for intellectual capability and that some races have higher aptitudes and so on.

The point is that if you follow Aristotle's line of thinking to its conclusion, a fundamental Aristotelian view, then the priority of the life of the intellectual is so firmly established that no other aspect of society will have any influence in reordering the priorities of human life. By this Sen means "that among this great clan there is the idea that there is no scope for political discussions at all." The priorities are already firmly set in stone.

This is where Sen departs from the historical Aristotelian positioning, as Sen believes that individuals living in a society have different needs and therefore different types of priorities. Therefore, when faced with the issue of scarcity and the choice of better food or shelter, one must confer with the individuals. The question as to how society decides what the priorities should be, is therefore a political question. The issues must be discussed with the individuals, as they will know the importance they attribute to the priorities. There is no forgone conclusion and therefore there is no escape that political dialogue is the process by which the just society as a whole must establish the freedom for each citizen to address these crucial concerns. For Sen, the re-ordering and prioritising of varying needs and values is such a deep seated process of individual human development that he repositions social choice theory as fundamental to the social economic analysis of underdevelopment.

'Social choice theory' is the manner in which the re-ordering of values is realized through the process of policy discussions. Inevitably individuals living in a particular society have different needs and different types of priorities and therefore development must enable their potential to obtain their choice and protect the process. Some critics of social choice theory question the viability of applying these ideals to projects on the ground. Yet the significance of social choice is that it provides the mechanism to expand current urban development objectives, beyond the obvious defini-tions of the five freedoms, to enable the capability of each individual to participate in the design and monitoring of urban development objectives. If we agree that 'development is freedom', then providing a method by which a society goes about deciding individual priorities must involve political freedoms. In Sen's view, the necessity of political dialogue is thus inescapable. The political process is something within which people can deal with issues, votes and have their views represented. For Sen politics is present and the question of re-ordering priorities is a political matter, depending on public discussions supported in large part by freedom of the media and press to provide the valid information to allow these discussions to take place and be shared locally, nationally and or even globally. In Sen's view, the priorities of freedoms have not been pre-determined or settled before either historically by Aristotle or in one of those divine philosophi-cal exercises like John Rawls, the original Position in some imagined primordial state. In Sen's opinion this is not how one goes about setting all these questions. On the contrary he explains,

> *"we do have to think of all society and freedom. If a society happened*
> *to adopt the position that there is a new set priorities, then it must be*
> *possible for public discussions to take place and arguments put*

forward and a decision reached. This is the process which is part of public reason."

Urban development policies would need to evaluate political freedoms by their success in re-ordering and by whether the political freedom has enhanced and protected the capability of individual social choice. Sen would say a broad level democratic choice, by which he does not mean only elections and votes, but crucially the ability to set up ongoing public discussions. Through public discussions there is a process of re-ordering of values that needs constant reinvesting with real experience. In Sen's opinion these public discussions are the microcosm of world public reason, which can resonate internationally and explains why contemporary culture and literature is important to us and of such value. He explained the aim of the Freedom Approach is to provide a way for people to look at problems of the human condition, the problems of world development and the problems of poverty.

Education and human development

Urban development objectives include providing the opportunity for schools and education. Access to education can be blocked by the absence of both the physical structure and of qualified teachers and texts. A whole range of issues is implicated in a schools project including the design of the building materials, health issues and orientation to other aspects of the community. With regard to the application of a Freedom Approach a school project would take a multi-objective direction based on the participation of the community. This may even include re-considering the qualitative merits of the school's curriculum with regard to the values of the community.

Education curricula have always identified the key subjects that provide the basic broad-based foundation to place young people successfully within a local, national and even global culture and community. The earliest concerns of educationalists faced fundamental discussions about the nature of human development in societies and the inherent linkages to human aspirations and freedom. Education curricula would include humanities, sciences, languages and practical education sources with the aim of giving birth to the ideal citizen. Clearly cultural heritage and national identity associations could coerce a curriculum that prompted loyalties to an invented national historical identity from a very young age. Religions or ideologies could provide compact solutions to the search for universal values and make these values seem to be permanent and absolutely above question. In this case the education system would be designed as a powerful central processor to iron out differences and emphasize the range of evaluations of various achievements on a common scale of marks. This approach became part of the twentieth century nation-building effort in which differences between communities or individuals were seen to be at odds with the idea of a common nationality and a shared patriotism. This profound trust of the nation as an upholder of the universal interests of all the citizens in a country is now beginning to change. Loyalties are increasingly being expressed around narrower definitions of identity. One only needs to consider the events that have fragmented the Soviet Union, Yugoslavia, Palestine and Israel to understand how differences seem to be the deciding factors for a sense of identity rather than the shared beliefs and interests.

An extreme example of a curriculum manipulating differences between citizens can be found in Dubai, United Arab Emirates. The subject of the Holocaust is not authorized teaching in history classes. The curriculum does not recognize the Holocaust ever took place nor does it recognize the state of Israel. In practical terms every book is reviewed and the subject of the Holocaust and Israel is deleted from all texts.

In favour of a more holistic curriculum in the USA, Senator Dede Alpert of California, announced the introduction of legislation that would require the development of a model curriculum on California Native American history and culture in April 2001. Senate Bill 41 required the Department of Education to request proposals for grants to develop model curricula, aligned with state content standards, on California Native American history, culture and tribal sovereignty, for pupils in grades 1 to 12. These grant requests would then be reviewed by a 14-member panel appointed by the Board of Education, the Governor, the Lieutenant Governor, the Speaker of the Assembly, Senate Rules Committee, and the State Librarian. At least five of the 14 members would represent California Native Americans, and a sixth member would represent the Native American Heritage Commission.

According to Senator Alpert, education about California Native Americans remains limited and out-of-date in spite of recent efforts made by public schools to recognize California's diversity. Far too often education focuses primarily on the culture and history of a few Indian nations and concludes in the early 1900s. Such an approach perpetuates stereotypes about Native Americans. 'In California there are more than 100 California Indian tribal governments,' Alpert said. 'It is time that the state develop a curriculum for its students that acknowledges Native American history, culture and tribal sovereignty in a comprehensive way.

However even in democratic countries, curricula and history can fluctuate according to which party is in power. For example in India, the new Congress-led government (elected in May 2004) is poised to rewrite the history books used to teach the nation's school children after a panel of eminent historians recommended scrapping text books written by scholars hand-picked by the previous Hindu nationalist administration (Ramesh 2004). According to Ramesh, 'Hundreds of thousands of textbooks are likely to be scrapped by the National Council of Education Research and Training, the central government body that sets the national curriculum for students up to 18.' To highlight the intensity of concern regarding the way history is portrayed in education curricula, this move of the new government to address the national education curriculum is its first initiative and strongly signals a departure from the programme of its predecessor. Critics of the last government, which was characterized by its religious fundamentalism and Hindu revivalists, 'depicted India's Muslim rulers as barbarous invaders and the medieval period as a dark age of Islamic colonial rule which snuffed out the glories of the Hindu empire that preceded it.' Several of India's outstanding examples of Islamic architecture were identified as Hindu commissions and designs, while the pernicious effects of the caste system had been downplayed. Many on the Hindu right are furious that their 'revisionist' interpretation of history is now being revised, blaming the influence of 'Leftists and Marxists'.

Several years ago the Ministry of Education of the Palestinian Authority in the Middle-East began to address the nature of problems for minority communities and how they had been denied access to basic educational facilities by a dominant majority. Denials of access to basic facilities for learning is one way in which the strong in a community are able to place obstructions in the path of the human development of the weak or the minority.

UNESCO identified representatives to work with the Ministry of Education of the Palestinian Authority during an eight-month period from September 1998 to April 1999. A special unit was established within the Ministry of Education to prepare a manual for norms and standards for school buildings that the ministry could use to standardize designs and reporting procedures as well as tenders. The outcome of this exercise was *Handbook 1998: Future Schools in Palestine: A Manual for Designing Schools* (Khosla 2000). This manual took into consideration the requirements of a new curriculum that had been prepared by the curriculum centre that UNESCO had help establish in the ministry.

Palestine has remained a failed idea and a failed state because they have been isolated not only by their neighbours but also by the rest of the world. The Palestinian Authority sought international help to define its future citizens through the educational process. Palestine has special problems of development and that means education. In the midst of conditions of a war zone, it has had no option but to define the educational syllabus with the intention of producing an ideal citizen who could use knowledge as a basis of matching his or her adversaries. From almost 100 per cent enrolment in Basic classes —about 750 000 students – the enrolment gets reduced to 60 000 at the secondary level, of whom some 16,000 fail. The Basic level classroom requirement is some 19 000 classrooms, while at the secondary level there is need for only some 2000. There was a need to define the basic parameters within which schools could be designed.

The handbook illustrated the changes to the curriculum that were introduced. Music and chants, agriculture, home economics and vocational education have been dropped as universal subjects. The classes and subjects proposed in the new curriculum have a direct relevance to the design of the schools. English has been introduced for the first time at Basic level. The number of weekly classes has been increased from 27 to 30. A free activity subject has been introduced requires new equipment to be installed to offer the student a range of options. Civics has been introduced as a new subject. It was interesting to note that almost 40 per cent of the classroom time was to be taken up by Islamic Studies, Arabic and English – a clear expression of the imagined identity of the future Palestinian. The need to re-define values and standards covers all issues relating to the education curriculum in Palestine, including a summary of furniture sizes, classroom layouts, school locations in relation to the community and so on.

When governments and legislation agree to drop the obsession with creating an imagined ideal human being, then deeper and more meaningful questions can be discussed in regard to the goals of education and human development theories. For example:

- How does one become aware, through a shared learning process, of the differences that exist between individuals?

- What are the kinds of differences between individuals that, if they manifest, will undermine the harmonious relationships between the members of a community?

- Is there a shared norm that the community endorses against which differences should be observed, respected and permitted?

- How does one distinguish between the universal and the particular in an individual's identity?

- How does one arrive at a judgement about a common curriculum that one should follow for a community when we know that there are enormous differences of identity and needs at the individual level?

These are crucial issues to consider because the answers to these questions lie at the heart of how one designs-in objectives for any development project that is, at one level, a central processor of universal identities and aspirations and, at another level, able to address the differing needs of the multiple ethnic communities.

Within this environment of denser and closer ethnic identity formations affecting cities globally, the problem confronting policy makers is how can one define the difference between what is universal and what is unique. By unique we mean factors that could be attributed to each individual's case including differences of personal characteristics, environmental backgrounds, social and climatic variations, as well as varying deprivations of learning and consumption.

While the provision of basic physical infrastructure facilities remains the concern of disempowered societies, the role of education as a universal aspiration addresses the differing needs of the multiple ethnic communities that make up the population of any city in any nation which has set out to form a universal education system. Thus urban development policy must facilitate wider participation and help individuals in a society to discover values that enable each of them to have a unique identity without being pressurized to conform to the values of a majority culture to which they may not belong.

In considering the applicability of the ideals set out in Sen's Freedom Approach, it may be necessary to consider evaluating and perhaps redefining the role of the community in the formulation of what constitutes the syllabus of a learning process. There needs to be a method which explores the way by which a democratic decision of a community defines what is to be universal and what is to be particular and a subject of choice. It should be possible to arrive at a community choice about what is regarded to be common to the whole community, forming the universal in the learning process, without restraining the varying interests of each of the individuals who constitute that community. One needs to ensure that group decisions about the universal content of a syllabus or learning mechanism do not become an inconsistent imposition that harms some minority.

- 9 -

The Role of Culture

"You thought you were a part, small, but in you there is a universe, the greatest." [12]

Consider the values that spring from within the citizen. They relate more to the rewarding satisfaction of exploring one's own potential and character. These are the values that provide guidelines to the intelligent, instinctive, emotional and spiritual realm that determines wisdom and ethical actions. These are the values that integrate social behaviour and structure in communities.

The choice that an individual makes about the life they choose to lead is strongly influenced by culture. Russian philologist Mikhail Bakhtin was perhaps the first theoretician to draw attention to this link. [13] He had emphasized the connections between the character and potential of a person and his cultural identity. In each culture, Bakhtin maintained, the past had enormous characteristics and potentials, which remain hidden, not revealed and unrealized. These are present throughout the history of that culture. The presence of an alien culture inevitably leads to new questions being asked about their own cultural identity. The alien culture too views the neighbouring culture as a whole, an entity, and the portrayal of deeper meanings begin to be discovered about the identity of both cultures. The ensuing dialogue between the two cultures does not result in a merger or mixture or blending of the two into one. Each culture reinforces and retains its own integral nature, unity and uniqueness so that both cultures get enriched. Conversely such a process could work the other way and cause deep and intense antagonism within an urban setting (This is certainly the case of Jerusalem). However when cultures demonstrate their ability to co-exist peacefully, the unity of shared respect works to maintain and enhance the potential of the entire human settlement and even the nation.

'Cultural traditions are understood as the presiding idea of a normal society and the animating principle of the whole life of a people,' (Ardalan 1973). Culture can inform the underlying physical designs of the built environment and determine the visual characteristics recognized in the vast diversity of vernacular and cultural traditions. Therefore an urban freedom development programme would expand the success of how cultural values are expressed, particularly in the spoken traditions which lie at the heart of social behaviour, knowledge and development initiatives. It would establish development objectives to encourage the often-ignored individual expressions of culture as vital for the dynamic of cities.

The fear that all cultural expressions are in some way imprisoned by static traditions with no mechanism for adjusting to modern life misses the point. According to Seyyed Hossein Nasr, in his Introduction to Ardalan's *The Sense of Unity*, the traditions of culture

> *"continues as long as the civilization which has brought it into being and the people for whom it is the guiding principle survive. And even when it ceases to exist outwardly, it does not die completely but returns to the universal origins from which it came".*

Ardalan, 1973

The validity of cultural expression will be valued by the quality of life the individual is enabled to choose and live. For these reasons Sen has focused his work on the freedoms of social choice and participation. Few economists can so substantially link the history of diverse cultural values to the entitlements of participation, freedom and democracy. He uses the word consequential, derived from the Latin, consequentia, meaning to 'follow closely', or from the philosophical doctrine of 'consequentialism', describing how the morality of an action is to be judged solely by its consequence.

Nasr argues as follows:

> *"Freedom alone without guiding ethics and values to guide meaningful action is capable of mass genocide. Ours is the only time in history in which human beings claim for themselves absolute rights with disrespect for the rest of creation. If absolute freedom and human rights means the right to actions that destroy the web of life on the planet, the dangers of freedom are much greater than the benefits."*

Nasr, 1999

Nasr's ardent concern with guiding ethics and values, is justified. In his opinion guiding ethics exist in every tradition and yet the process by which they are experienced and reinvest the present and the future with meaning has not be recognised in development policy. Ironically this is the same source from which human aspirations for a good life are born. For these reasons Nasr would argue that guiding ethics need continued and even greater emphasis in development policy in order to guide social agency directions. Continual participation is essential in order to keep the ongoing dialogue of human ethics at the forefront of all decision-making. If the consequence of an urban development initiative has not achieved what the people need to be well and live the life they value, (and that includes management of the earth's resources vital for human habitats and all living creatures) then there is a need to ensure the values and the process that determine principles of more humanity and responsibility are made accessible The question facing development policy makers is how can this be achieved?

For Sen these concerns are vital-and central to his own work as the Nobel economist who places such an emphasis on the concept of Freedom. So it comes as no surprise to find, at the heart of his book, *Development as Freedom*, the ancient story of Emperor Ashoka who lived in the third century BC. Sen retells the story in the his chapter Culture and Human rights:

> *"[Ashoka] commanded the largest empire of all the Indian Kings (including the Mughals and even the Raj). He turned his attention to the concerns of public ethics and enlightened politic after witnessing the horrific carnage of his own victorious battle against the Kingdom of Kalinga (what is now Orissa). He converted to Buddhism, and not only helped to make it a world religion by sending emissaries abroad with the Buddhist message to east and to west, but also covered the country with stone inscriptions describing forms of good life and the nature of good government. The inscriptions give a special importance to tolerance of diversity. For example the edict (now numbered X11) at Erraguidi."*

> Sen, 1999

Likened to an early National Recovery Programme, Ashoka's objectives were quite simple and could be summed up as the desire to assist his citizens to recover a sense of morality, respect and tolerance – even for the perpetrator who had caused such suffering. Nonetheless Akhoka did not have to hand the extensive media facilities available in our twenty-first century to share out these ideals. Communications were limited to the oral tradition, symbols and words skilfully crafted into distinguishing features in the built environment and stone inscriptions.

Remarkably Ashoka foresaw the need to encourage individual agency and participation between the diversity of cultural groups. The aim was not, as we have referred to earlier 'a merger or mixture or blending of the two into one'. The intention was for each culture to reinforce and retain its own integral nature, unity and uniqueness so that both cultures would be enriched and respectful to the other. In this case, Ashoka referred to the Buddhist teachings but relied on citizens as the agents of change to establish public discussions between themselves. He believed the action of making these values accessible allowed people to think intelligently and to be free to make choices that would ultimately both relieve the suffering of the people and further the dynamic of social economic security and quality of life across his empire.

Stone sculpture of
the Buddha,
India.

(Mike Ryan)

*"A man must not do reverence to his own sect or disparage that of
another man without reason. Depreciation should be for specific
reason only, because the sects of other people all deserve reverence for one reason or another. By thus acting a man exalts his
own sect, and at the same time does service to the sects of other
people. By acting contrariwise, a man hurts his own sect, and
does disserve to the sects of other people. For he who does reverence to his own sect while disparaging the sects of others wholly
from attachment to his own, with intent to enhance the splendour
of his own sect, in reality by such conduct inflicts the severest
injury on his own sect."*

King Ashoka, XIIth Edict of Erraguidi[14]

In our current time, technological advanced communication provides the possibility to unite diverse cultures. Yet it has not proved successful against growing cultural conflicts and warfare affecting major historic centres across the world. On the one hand the multi-layered complexity of cultural conflicts can wipe out years of seemingly successful international development initiatives, while on the other the ancient words of Ashoka's edicts have survived and continue to be retold 1800 years later. Thus cultural wisdom has the potential to provide solutions. We can now return to Sen who explains:

> *"The exercise of all freedoms is mediated by values, but the values in turn are influenced by public discussions and social interactions, which are themselves influenced by participatory freedoms. These values can influence the freedoms that people enjoy and have reason to treasure and can influence social features such as gender equity, the nature of childcare, family size, fertility patterns and the treatment of the environment. Prevailing values can also affect the presence or absence of corruption and the role of trust in economic, social or political relationships."*

Sen, 1999

Cultural values cannot function without the freedom of ongoing participation, discussion and expression. Here lie the roots of cultural conflicts as, significantly, values are passed on in spoken words, oral folk stories, rituals and cultural expressions. Conflicts arise when obstructions to cultural expression have been overlooked and dismissed without understanding their links to the individual's well-being and citizenship.

Culture without ethics

A recent review of a favela slum community in Rio de Janeiro, Brazil, identifies over 500 individuals who were initially interviewed 30 years earlier. The report confirms a substantial growth of slum populations. The more disturbing feature, however, is the self-assessment of the 'very poor'. Over the 30-year period they had acquired basic assets including shelter, water and light only to realize their lives were empty of quality and they still consider themselves very poor. According to Perlman (2002) the people feel "overwhelmingly that they do not earn enough to live a dignified life". A significant percentage of those interviewed did earn the minimum necessary for a decent life so money was not the real issue. 'Something else is going on that makes this population feel they have lost ground and that the gap between the rest of society and themselves has widened.' Through a series of interviews the conclusions of the report identified the growing influence of modern communication and the media image of worldwide consumer standards depicting a culture of affluence.

The following explanation by Alberto Lopes, an urban planner and researcher at the Brazilian Institute of Municipal Administration (IBAM) represents Sen's ideas and gives a broad perspective to his experience of the favelas.

The overexposure of the favelas in Rio de Janeiro to violence has reanimated the debate on what must be done. Old ideas have come back while new ones try to impose themselves. The long-term government policies 'obrismo' emphasising physical interventions, promised redemption to the favelas.[15] Meanwhile their inhabitants fight for major communication space in the media so as to spread what they believe about themselves and what they have accomplished in a number of cultural and social initiatives so far.

The favelas have been born out of deprivation and have increasingly developed as an urban phenomenon. There is the political expectation that the favela will eventually shape itself into a formal neighbourhood, in contrast to what happens in the central modernized areas of the city where the ethics of a re-creation process speedily reaches it goal. It goes without saying that we can no longer legitimize the thinking of past development projects addressing poverty as an epiphenomenon. The question now facing public policy is a re-ordering of values that can broaden the social horizons of the down-trodden.

For example, the value of water is now considered a global strategic asset, as its value is heightened by it scarcity. Even so families that have water provision at their doors would rather look for alternative sources so as to get away with not paying the consumption bill. They also 'tap' electrical energy and cable TV networks. Activities like these provide evidence that the expansion of material consumption in the poor areas does not correspond to the promotion of ethics and citizenship values. Consumers are forged without producing citizens.

We are faced with the question as to how to dismantle the geography of drug trafficking inside the favela considering that its internal organization has adjusted itself to the militarization of the drug business in the settlement. We cannot avoid the fact that schools and day-care centres are not allowed to work and that houses, sometimes associated with public investments, are incorporated into the assets and functioning of drug trafficking. Every effort to respond to social tensions has been insufficient in establishing a social environment that will achieve greater social productivity and performance of the cities.

Throughout time, housing projects such as 'City of God' – built to shelter favela populations (and separated from the dignified areas of the city) – have been shown to be even more oppressive places than the slums

Rio de Janeiro
viewed from a
Favela.

(Jon Spaull/
Panos)

they intended to replace. Anyone who visits City of God, even after the film's four nominations for the Oscar Academy Awards, is able to witness how the growing number of modifications to the original project reflect the barriers imposed on the freedom of the inhabitants and to their process of social and economic inclusion in life of the city. Carlos Nelson Ferreira dos Santos has preached the exercise of a para-architecture and a metalanguage for the craft of architects in these areas.

For Amartya Sen, poverty must be seen as deprivation of capabilities, instead of low levels of income. Therefore, it is not easy to respect the liberal thesis that attributes the causes of poverty and social immobility to indolence. Sen provides an alternative to the thesis of 'making the cake to eventually share it' and to strategic promises that restore the healthier ones while the weaker ones die off.

Any favela dweller looks forward to improvements of their housing conditions, since it can dignify them as a citizen and facilitate their bonds with the city. However, these dwellers have also stated that the mere physical intervention cannot change the favela. They are quite aware that citizenship has to do not only with their fixed addresses but also with investing in their own character and potential. They have been pointing out allies that can address the obstructions hindering a more creative cultural and articulate participation in the organization of the city. It is up to us to open flanks where human freedoms can be expanded and to affirm a sociable environment. We must provide sustainability to development where the process of addressing the physical needs of the people have not facilitated individual civil rights and citizenship.

Alberto Lopes 2004

The poverty described by Lopes is not defined by classic economic measurements but culturally imposed social poverty. The favela could be characterized by the absence of what culture would provide in terms of social tools to re-craft relevant ethics in light of changing times. A Removing Unfreedoms urban recovery programme for the favelas would encourage the participation that guarantees the individual freedom to recreate and recognize their contribution to citizenship and sense of place in their city.

Although policy makers are aware that communication and local knowledge figures highly in cultural communities, there is little evidence of measuring the obstructions to cultural wisdom that lays the foundation for citizenship within diverse human settlements. Alternative evaluations need to measure the individual freedom to participate in cultural expressions that provide opportunities to source ethical values and restore individual potentials and capabilities.

Mixed migrant communities

Urban communities include mixed migrant populations where daily life is no longer integrated with many of the cultural expressions and attributes associated with a functioning historical cultural identity. These absent traits include a recognized shared history; geography or a cohesive social structure connected to spiritual values and belief systems. The urban migrant population is physically, ideologically and emotionally dislocated from its previous geographical and social character and begins to adopt a new cultural identity that is formulated in response to the role of the dominant culture into whose domain they have migrated. As Hulya Turgut explains, the integration with the city life may take the form of a series of processes, which reflect physical and socio-cultural characteristics of the past cultural identity. Important changes may begin to take place in their lifestyles and aspirations with reference to a new cultural identity as they experience urbanization as an inflexible collection of interactive exterior forces (Turgut 1990).

It may be that the migrant population has recently escaped an oppressive social or political situation, or abandoned a failing rural economy. Nevertheless 'acculturation patterns' of migrant populations in urban settings have been shown initially to reflect the physical and socio-cultural characteristics of the region from which they have migrated. In these initial instances a cultural memory is functioning and forms part of the specific identity of the group. During the continued process of 'acculturation' previous cultural values and ties get weaker and may even disappear so that the urban settlements transform and reformulate a new set of complex relationships determined by exterior forces and a new preference of lifestyle. Under the external influences there are unyielding pressures to adopt new values or to assimilate others. While many cultural traits have been remarkably persistent in a period of great technological and political change, others have been devalued, often with damaging results to both rural and urban aspirations and environments.

Consistently the primary vehicle for both the transference of cultural knowledge and the creation of new aspirations takes place verbally, whether consciously or not. Another method is through the physical body memory process characteristic of many cultures. Both the individual and collective experience of the spoken word originates in the memory realm of the collective consciousness of the people. This can be rooted to the previous geographical home of the migrant people but, nevertheless, the spoken word is a fundamental characteristic in shaping and preserving cultural identity. The circumstances under which new quality of life aspirations arise need to be considered by urban development initiatives in culturally dislocated migrant populations. Hidden cultural characteristics may migrate into the informal city by way of a spoken folk memory and express themselves or remain silent. The degree to which this memory is set in motion determines the expression of the cultural identity in relation to the formal city or the new environment.

Indicators need to consider both the constraints and capabilities of cultural values and how they may become part of new reference values within urban development policies.

The oral unwritten folk tradition explained by Julie Cruikshank is not so much the same story of a past geographical identity but a present evolving awareness with ongoing ideas, continually reinvested with new meaning (Cruikshank 1992).

Good and best practices in different cultural contexts

To assist migrant populations to take part in policy-led urban initiatives aimed at eliminating poverty, a recent DFID report has idenitified how best to communicate good and best practices in different cultural contexts (DFID 2002). However, a further objective, in keeping with freedom-centred priorities, could be to work to identify and remove the unfreedoms which block the potentials of the individual to restore their cultural identity in the new urban setting.

A key feature of the DFID study emphasizes the role of networks in encouraging broader concepts of social capital, in sharing and generating new knowledge and in adapting best or good practices. The report proposes the need for key representative members and their gatekeepers to be identified, with the help of community representatives and intermediaries such as NGOs, CBOs, local universities and government. The suggestion is that through the gatekeeper it will become easier to understand what these urban communities need and how the local cultural groups gain access to the knowledge necessary to realize their potentials. Central to this process is the recognition that these communities have their own local knowledge which forms an integral part of everyday practices but is not learned in a formal setting. By building on this initiative it would be possible to expand the role of the gatekeeper and identify the obstructions to social agency within Sen's five-freedoms framework. The gatekeeper would support the participatory process necessary to increase the community's capability for self-governance.

Cultural conflicts

There are many cases where the diverse cultures in urban environments have shared and developed worthwhile, indispensable and flourishing habitat strategies. Jewelled moments of cultural renaissance and heritage testify to these multi-ethnic assemblies across civilization. However, the history of religious, tribal and cultural relationships provides numerous examples of cultural clashes within a single nation. Perhaps the most dramatic event of cultural communalism in the past century is that of the partition of India, which left both India and Pakistan devastated. A current example, of lesser proportions, is the city of Nicosia in Cyprus, which was divided 30 years ago when a Greek-Cypriot coup prompted an invasion by Turkish troops. Since 1974's bloody events, a United Nations-patrolled buffer zone has divided Cyprus in two – with the divide running right through Nicosia. The buffer zone both protects the citizens of each culture and, in the process, isolates the now silent empty buildings and streets, overgrown by slender trees and walled off by barbed wire, large metal drums and sandbags. This is Europe's last divided capital. Although this is indeed an extreme example, current cultural conflicts within urban communities across the globe precipitate a growing concern. Recurrent repressive relationships are evident where the stronger community uses its power to enforce economic constraints on the less strong population.

A study by Frances Stewart unravels the complexity of obstructions that beset individuals who are forced to endure culturally imposed poverty (Stewart 2002). An important factor in multi-cultural and multi-ethnic communities that distinguishes the violent examples from the peaceful is the existence of 'severe multi-dimensional inequalities between culturally defined groups'. These inequalities are generated not solely by economic advantage but more often than not by distinguished cultural belief systems and ideologies that highlight differences. The inequalities become more obvious for the deprived population and the wealth increases for the advantaged. The resulting deprivations can be shockingly severe, taking centuries

Divided Cities.
The Green Line,
which divides
Nicosia, Cyprus in
two with barriers
erected across the
street, viewed
from the south
side.

(George
Georgiou/
Panos)

to resolve as in the case of slavery and apartheid. Deprivations include
substantially reduced incomes, reduced access to education, higher illiteracy
levels, ineffectual land reforms, political exclusion, absent medical care and
higher infant mortality rates. The resentment of the deprived can push
desperate individuals towards joining fundamentalist group. The 'us or
them' terrorism tactics are illustrated in several of the eight case studies
considered by Stewert. Most unsettling of the current terrorism campaigns
are the dark waves of suicide bombers in the Middle East. These young men
and women sacrifice their youth for martyrdom, destroying themselves and
innocent lives, based on interpretations of the Koran. Their actions have led
the Israeli government to build a 788-kilometre barrier as a non-violent
defensive measure, which has dramatically reduced attacks by Palestinians
in areas where it has been completed. However, the International Court of
Justice in The Hague ruled (10 July 2004) that Israel's West Bank security
barrier breaches international law and should be dismantled. Nonetheless,
Israel has argued that the Court has no jurisdiction in the matter and will
ignore the issue.

When a culturally defined group is isolated by imposed severe inequalities, all members take on a distinct exaggerated collective identity that
demands that the individual forfeit freedoms of individual potential and
capability. They become the Blacks, the Poor, the Protestants, the Jews, the
Moslems, the Catholics, or the Palestinians. The affluent cultural groups in

conflict exaggerate their ideological justification in order to advance their group influence. However, in reality, if circumstances of severe inequalities persist, the entire economic stability of the nation suffers. Many examples exist where conflict populations of the 'Middle City' are forced to endure the equivalent of prison camp existences where mafia economies continually sabotage any effort to restore or secure livelihoods.

When considering the predicted global population increase – over two billion new urban residents over the next 30 years – there exists a very real possibility that the influx of migrant populations could further increase active cultural inequalities within populations. This is already evident in major cities in developed countries as in the example of the Black population in the city of London. There exists 'a major source of resentment among black youths arising from the fact that they are five times more likely to be stopped and searched by police than whites and four times more likely to be arrested,' (Stewart 2002).

The inequalities and poverty imposed on the Palestinians by Israel is a topical example where military dictates, rather than market forces, regulate the economy. Water is a natural resource that is a primary necessity for basic survival – particularly in the Middle-East where its scarcity heightens its value even further. Recently Turkey has agreed to a new pipeline that will supply water to the Middle-East. However the issue of equal distribution to the Palestinians is being monitored by international

Divided Cities. Palestinian women and a child stand next to the controversial separation wall in the West Bank suburb of Jerusalem, Abu Dis, which is being cut off from the city by the wall.

(Chryssa Panoussiadou/ Panos)

humanitarian organizations. Palestinians applying for a licence to dig a well requires eighteen approvals. This process can take up to five years before the well is available for use. In these circumstances the Palestinian agricultural-based economy is severely curtailed. 'Such use of an economic resource for ideological purposes has naturally distorted the economies of both communities,' (Khosla 2002).

Solutions to multi-layered conflicts are not easy to come by. This is not due to lack of effort by international mediators or even to a lack of Nobel Prize citations. In the case of Israel and Palestine the list of peace plans, initiatives and analysis fill entire sections of international policy libraries. Setting laws and even enforced regulations has not produced the desired results.

In the case of religious conflicts in India, the new Congress-led government has plans to introduce a law to protect religious minorities (July 2004). The idea of new legislation to deal with communal violence was first mentioned by President Abdul Kalam, when he addressed the new Indian parliament following national elections in April and May. Interior minister Shivraj Patil explains the law would target those who instigated, abetted or funded unrest. 'We will definitely not tolerate it.' The decision by the new Congress-led government to enforce regulations is in reaction to the wake of riots that broke out in the western state of Gujarat in 2002, in which more than 1,000 people died, most of them Muslim. The proposed law would spell out the role of the federal government and the states in addressing unrest. 'It will be a law which will really deal with communal violence,' (BBC 2004).

Although it is hard to believe that the new law will encourage the values of the previous Bharatiya Janata Party to change over night, the suffering caused by enforced cultural inequities will no doubt be curtailed. Yet the long-term solution has not been addressed. The question as to what can be done to heal the lives and remove the unfreedoms of both the victims and perpetrators of such long-term, deep-set cultural antagonism has not been addressed. According to Emperor Ashoka, and indeed the arguments put forward by Amartya Sen, more participation is needed and more public discussion must be encouraged. There is a growing opinion within international agencies, particularly UNESCO and the EU, that communities characterized by differing cultural and religious values must speak to each other and that intercultural and interfaith participation dialogue is the vital antidote to conflict and the long-term urban recovery solution for peace. According to the Nobel Peace Prize recipient, His Holiness the Dalai Lama of Tibet, legislation and national agreements by themselves do not re-align the positioning of individuals who for several generations have been tormented, pressurized, polarized and entrenched in ethnic differences. The religions must speak to each other with respect and compassion.[16]

Removing unfreedoms

A unique and courageous attempt to implement community participation dialogue is currently being undertaken by the Interfaith Encounter Association (IEA) in Israel. The IEA operates within three concentric circles of interfaith work each with the power to grow and impact the circle encapsulating it. In the first and most pre-eminent circle – the Inner-Israeli circle – the IEA focuses on the promotion of respectful relations between Jews, Muslims, Christians, Druze and Baha'is living in Israel. This process in turn impacts and enables the second circle – the Israeli-Palestinian circle – where, until the current intifada, the IEA worked in cooperation with five Palestinian organizations across the Palestinian National Authority (PNA). The work of the first and second circles aids the work of the third circle – the Middle-East region – where the IEA has been a major founder in establishing the Middle-East Abrahamic Forum, along with similar organizations from Cyprus, Egypt, Jordan and the PNA. The IEA is guided by the following basic principles and goals:

- equal representation of all faiths; equality of the genders
- outreach to individuals from all faiths, age groups, walks of life and levels of society
- outreach to individuals across the religious–secular and political spectrums
- continual recruitment through committed activists
- implementation of interactive programs that effectively change outlooks and attitudes, such as extended weekend seminars and ongoing study groups
- continual development of new models for effective encounter
- ongoing evaluation of all strategies and programs.

According to Yehuda Stoluv, the founder of the IEA:

"The vision is a society in which the 'otherness' of the other is not only accepted, but understood. The IEA believe that, rather than being the cause of the problem, culture and religion should be the solution to the conflicts that exist in the Middle-East region and beyond. We do not believe in the blending of all traditions into one undifferentiated group, but in providing a table where all can come and sit in safety and ease, while being fully who they are in their respective religions."

The IEA includes over 4000 associates and sends weekly email newsletters internationally documenting every encounter meeting each week. Their methodology is to take the varying stories of the different culture and religions and, issue by issue, compare and understand the differences.

Currently the administrators of the IEA are designing a project based on Sen's Freedom Approach and the individual as the agent of change. The project will evaluate and monitor how individuals within the different faiths achieve the lifestyle they value leading by mapping the process of cultural expressions and individual social decision making. The project would then serve to appreciate how the Jews, Muslims, Christians, Druze and Baha'is view the principle process of development. The participants would submit the results of their encounters to a common evaluation procedure and, through aggregating the listing in the five-freedoms framework make observable the success of interfaith participation activities to national, international and city-to-city global governance programmes.[17]

Understanding culturally imposed differences and inequalities, between one cultural group and another, is a neglected area in urban development initiatives. Adopting the five-freedoms development framework would identify both the obstructions and the solutions necessary to restore the individual livelihoods of those suffering from cultural clashes and constraints. The effectiveness lies both in the respective roles of each freedom and their interconnections: 'The linkages tie the distinct types of freedom together in order to promote overall freedoms of people to lead the kind of lives they have reason to value,' (Sen 1999).

Cultural constraints for women

The opportunities for a woman to choose a quality of life worth living are often, more than any other group, constrained by cultural values. Some policy makers might say the gender issue has been addressed as its profile has been at the forefront of political discussion in developed countries for the past century. However the extent of cultural influences on women's ability to lead the life they value varies enormously between different cultural groups. Because of this the far-reaching impact and importance of women's contribution to human development has not been fully realized nor guaranteed.

In the slums of Mumbai, India, a group of women pavement dwellers have taken the initiative to begin a savings scheme. In many cases the husband, as the main income earner, has a very low self-esteem and diverts his worries to alcohol and gambling leaving no prospects of acquiring a home for the family. The women have focused more clearly on the need for investment. Each day one member volunteers to collect money from each participant. They call themselves the Mahila Milan (Women Together) Women's Savings Group. Their aim is that, over time, each woman will successfully save enough to build a home for their family.

Mahila Milan has been a local knowledge initiative. It came about with the support of the NGO SPARC and was facilitated through informal discussions within the women's group. The women have found their words and their values and have taken action to expand their capabilities. The savings scheme has created the space they needed outside the dominant cultural role. A more thorough Freedom analysis of their work will be described in a later chapter..

Culture and mortality

One example where the aftermath of a cultural conflict causes increased mortality for women has been highlighted internationally since the bombing of Afghanistan. Women living in Islamic cultures are not usually free to see male doctors and traditionally these women were attended by other women. Without access to modern medical attention and basic sterile practices, the women face much greater suffering than the men in the region as the female doctors are not as numerous as male ones, and the chances of a woman recovering from illness or injury are significantly lower. Culturally sensitive solutions have been devised to encourage the female birth attendants – otherwise known as traditional birth attendants (TBAs) – to have more access to medical knowledge and skills. By identifying individual needs, cultural constraints for women surface and become apparent, as do the solutions.

HIV/AIDS

Cultural indicators have also become apparent when addressing the issues of HIV/AIDS. The joint UNESCO/UNAIDS research project was launched in May 1998, with the aim of stimulating reflection and action for better application of 'a cultural approach' in strategies, policies, projects and fieldwork. This strategy engages populations in the fight against HIV/AIDS on the basis of their own cultural references and resources (UNESCO 1998). In terms of HIV/AIDS prevention and care, adopting a cultural approach means that any given population's cultural references and resources – ways of life, value systems, traditions, beliefs, religions and fundamental human rights – will be considered as key reference points when designing, implementing and monitoring prevention and care strategies, programmes and projects. Through understanding cultural values, development initiatives can encourage people's behaviour and thus give full coherence to preventive education, medical treatment, and proved care and support of infected and affected people

Evaluations and indicators

The goal of every policy maker is to create an enabling environment in which people's capabilities can be enhanced and their range of choices expanded.' Urban development initiatives must set up a modified information base that is sensitive to both the constraints and potentials of culture. New evaluations and new indicators are needed to measure the contributions culture makes in addressing the priorities of human development objectives across the world. Two key components need to be considered in re-ordering the value of cultural expressions to international urban development policy makers:

- Urban policy must identify the diversity and character of local cultures of the middle city.

- Urban policy needs to determine how it can enable the strengths of local cultures to introduce their own human values and vibrant economies into the community.

Indicators would measure the individual's ability to take part in dialogues he or she values and likewise meaningful rituals that ensure participation in the entire human life cycle including births, initiations, marriages and death. The obstructions to cultural expressions would be made observable through monitoring the participation process through the 5-freedom framework. In this way the communication of values and ethics will become the asset of cultural heritage spurred forward into the present and future. Citizens' capabilities and potentials are realised while protecting the ability to aspire for a future worth living.   Therefore the answer to the question does culture matter is answered convincingly by Arjun Appadurai:

> *"It is in culture that ideas of the future, as much as of those about the past, are embedded and nurtured. Thus, in strengthening the capacity to aspire, conceived as a cultural capacity, especially among the poor, the future-oriented logic of development could find a natural ally, and the poor could find the resources required to contest and alter the conditions of their own poverty."* [17]

Local knowledge, words of culture and tradition provide the continuity of values and enable each individual to come to know who they are, where they have come from and where they are going. Throughout history cultural and religious practices relate to worship and mark the progression of human life at a point where the external, spatial organization of the land and the inner human potential are connected and reflect a spiritual awareness (Oliver 1977). Of urgency is the increase in culturally imposed inequalities worldwide. To these ends urban policy makers must look with greater depth into alternative measures and identify the characteristics that are seen to be relevant.

- 10 -

Rethinking Project Design

We have not yet found a country-wide policy which gives the social commitment to the Freedom Approach and addresses the wide spectrum of obstructions that Sen specifies must be removed. Generally developed countries tend to focus partly on a donor's agenda while national governments tend to be guided by the planning commission or some such establishment, which inevitably narrows down the focus of the objectives.

The nature of the emergency in the Balkans, for example, tended to narrow down the areas of development action which were required, simply because the subject of economic insecurity and low employment focused too narrowly on one problem. In contrast The Freedom Approach suggests a much more holistic approach to development and asks us to question whether it is justifiable to have an emergency programme or any quick-fix programme? We must question programmes that alleviate things in the short term but actually do not address the underlying social obstructions or takes the community forward any faster in the long term.

So how does one connect Sen's theoretical discourse on development goals to the ground level reality of projects? In the case of the Freedom Approach, it so far remains largely unexplored on the ground. In order to take the development objectives of the Freedom Approach as a project goal, projects need to be designed in a different way. Projects are the instruments through which development initiatives are delivered. There is an important link between giving the five freedoms substance on the ground and the stages of the project cycle that hopes to deliver its developmental objectives.

Any project cycle has four main stages:

- Defining the context or framework for the approach.

- Identifying the problem and designing the project.

- Planning and implementation of the activities that compose the project.

- Monitoring, evaluating and assessing the impact of those activities.

Defining the context

Context defines the location of the project in the wider development arena not only of the country but also within the landscape of the surrounding socio-political, economical and cultural environment. In designing a project that will remove unfreedoms, it is important that the context is defined in such a way that primacy is given to the community and to the five interlinked development objectives which are defined within the constraints and obstructions at the national, group or collective level and individual level.

When describing the context of the socio-political landscape, both the existing knowledge and skills base of the community and the households must be considered as well as the ways it can be strengthened changed or given commercial opportunities. Possibilities for self-management must be defined based on the capabilities of individuals and the steps needed to enable this to take place.

In defining obstructions, we will need to identify both gross level and micro-level obstructions within the five-freedoms framework. Gross level obstructions affect the community as a whole and the role that authorities play must be recognized. Micro-level obstructions, on the other hand, affect different individuals in a community in different ways and need a range of solutions that should be defined in the project activities. Obstructions can come from within the households, from the community or from the state.

Identifying the problem and designing the project

The project design, at this stage of the cycle, will define the nuts and bolts objectives and the activities to reach those objectives. At this stage, a distinction will be made between the macro-obstructions that are shared by the community as a whole, such as land tenure or lack of infrastructure or environmental hazards, and the micro-obstructions that affect each member of the community in different ways. The project activities do not give priority to macro-obstructions over micro-obstructions. The lack of drinking water for the community is as important a constraint as the inability of one carpenter in the community to find work or the inability of a girl to be educated because of household attitudes. The Freedom Approach is a style of reasoning whereby you take into account the basic human parameters. Speaking at the July 2003 colloquium at LSE, Sen explained there are three points to consider.[19]

First, Amartya Sen advises to look at human beings, rather than systems and not to be influenced by a system that has a sound financial foundation or a sound market economy. 'You want to see how the lives of human beings are involved.'

Second, Sen explains that the method by which you can gain a greater understanding of the people is by looking at the values important in their lives, some of which, objectively, are very widely shared. In the discussion of universal needs he refers to the need for shelter as opposed to what type of shelter. Clearly one must distinguish the universal characteristics from the individual varying values and find out what importance the people attach to their values? A consideration in determining the importance of values is to identify how far gender issues affect the extent to which people have the opportunity to consider the evaluation. The ability to perceive whether there is inequality or not is dramatically important to Sen's criteria.

On this point, he refers to his work on famine in 1943 with health surveys taking place in an area not very far from Calcutta. One of the early works on health perception was to consider the features found in an area where a lot of people had suffered and a lot of people had relations that had died, because the famine killed so many people. When determining the level of health of these people several varying criteria were considered. For example, one criterion used by doctors at that time, directly asked 'is there something wrong?' In their diagnosis the doctor's results provided a list of a variety of ailments such as diabetes or heart problems or some other diagnosable feature. Another category was defined in terms of 'are you in poor health?' "The results to this category of questioning came back with 43 per cent of men saying they were in poor health. When the same question was asked to women the percentage of women who considered themselves in poor health was exactly zero." [19]

Sen explains that these results might lead you to conclude that women were in excellent health compared to men. Or it might lead you to reconsider and question the possibility that the women have no illness, or perhaps women had been 'trained' not to grumble. "Perhaps they think that ill health is something unseemly so not to be spoken of." [19] Or is it the case, as Sen's anthropological colleagues were saying, that the women have no concept of being an individual. According to Sen this interpretation "does not necessarily mean that such a concept of individual awareness does not exist for the Indian women, but that the reasoning to understand the concept of freedom had been denied to them." [19]

To further emphasize the importance of determining greater human parameters in development policy, Sen described his concern with the current international focus on the field of health and the macro-economic approach to health as discussed by Jeffrey Sachs (Sachs 2002). He described Sach's report as highlighting a variety of reasons why the market economy is inefficient and why we need many more public initiatives. Why, for instance, the richer countries have considerable obligations to poorer ones and why the AIDS epidemic and others like TB, malaria, etc. require greater attention. A higher health standard would save money that is wasted on many related health aspects, which need to be considered in order to stabilise national economies. However Sen followed through on his own analysis of the report and suggests that if we are to review the report and ask the question 'what is the justification of good health?', we would find the justification is that better health makes the economy grow faster and therefore incomes will be higher. Sen views this conclusion as the ridiculous that goes with the sublime. If there is anything in the Freedom Approach which clearly establishes the principles of what Sen is aiming to achieve, it is to get the priorities right. 'In this case to judge income for what it does to provide good health not judge health for what it does to your income.' [19]

Those who design and manage urban development projects may face a similar situation when an evaluator comes from outside with different criteria that do not identify the real priorities. Sen offered an insight into how the macro-economist Jeffrey Sachs and others anticipated a conflict of criteria. He believes that rather than trying to challenge the main dialogue, Sachs and his colleagues expanded this discussion on health and income to say: "If you believe income is important, let us tell you that health is important too." [19] The real feat, according to Sen, is that all those working in the area of health and development policy must be able to make distinctions between health and income.

> *"Health is important in itself. Human life is important and health is important. Then, you can say, as a matter of fact, if you are interested in income, it follows that health is important to income. There are two distinct points to be made and this is the most important sight we should not overlook."* [19]

Finally, the third point. It is Sen's view that if we follows the analysis and discover the context in which a Freedom Approach project could be formulated, we will never get a magic fail-safe repeatable design formula that will determine what freedoms are more important in every context. In his words, "there is not going to be a lazy solution to it. It has to be hard empirical work as to what is being overlooked, what is it that appears peculiar, how we could square it with the basic insight that we have and then to look for a solution." [19]

In conclusion a freedom-based approach is no more than an approach in that if you implement certain activities in light of this approach, what you do concretely in one situation may be very different from what you do in another situation. Developmental freedom is being able to generate from your individual and collective action and analysis of the context what is most appropriate for that situation.

Planning and implementation

The project activities that are identified in the previous stage have here to be put into action. It may be part of the project strategy to start with something small like a savings circle. Such an activity may give rapid results that are tangible in the eyes of the community. Alternatively, there may be another way to form a collective to enhance inter-community communication. Some sort of group formation initiatives could be taken at this stage to list individual as well as community obstructions. Strategies for removing obstructions in all the five domains of unfreedoms would be elaborated in this section.

Implementation is a complex part of the project stage because we are expecting to initiate actions at macro (community) level as well as micro (individual) level and address actions in all the five domains of unfreedoms. We are dealing with individual obstructions that have macro, meso and micro causes. For instance, in assessing the obstructions to social facilities, we may find that an individual may be prevented from gaining education because of an absence of schools in the area, or the wrong medium of education in a community or because the father does not agree to educate a child.

How you implement the Freedom Approach is not determined by one person, agency or institution. The design of the implementation process is very specific to the community. According to Desai you obviously want to be clear headed about what the approach signifies. We would need to identify characteristics in one space, or capability and so on. But the specific methods of implementing the project should be determined by the individuals participating in a process of dialogue. That is part of the re-ordering process and how collective action is decided. The implementation of the project will be decided as an outcome of participation and re-ordering of needs.

'This is a challenge to our current development framework. The Freedom Approach does not give targets or formulas and is open-ended and undetermined. When encountering a bear in a forest there is no survival code of action that you repeat in each instance,' explained Desai, 'One doesn't suddenly say do it this way and then one will survive, it's not like that. The Freedom Approach can be seen as an enabling instrument for urban development objectives.'[20]

Desai explained that if an approach is seen to be enabling by a mature community in which you are constructing this work, then it is like our understanding of morality. Morality nowadays will say whatever 'consenting' adults do is all right. Therefore as long as consenting adults say that this is the way we want to tackle our problem of dwelling, or whatever it is, then it is all right. 'What is important is that we realize our freedoms together, actively. The Freedom Approach is an idea and ideas change the world. What the work and re-ordering of poverty and famine has done is to give people a different way to look at the world. The world is the same, the world has not changed, but we see it in a different way. And that opens out possibilities. It doesn't close possibilities. One must never think of the Freedom Approach as closing off options. Because that would be a disservice.' [20]

When considering implementation, according to Sen, there will always be different levels of application. We have discussed dealing with habitat and with the context of habitats you will operationalize the approach in a certain way. In the context of relief other aspects will be considered. He explains that depending on the context and on the location it is necessary to think about these issues differently. The capability would depend upon the nature of the exercise but ultimately we are concerned with freedom. In Sen's opinion we will not prioritize high gross national product objectives for a market economy strategy even though we don't know what the social outcome will be. The social outcome is addressed from the start. According to Sen "the applicability of the approach has to be seen as something that affects the life of human beings and what better way than to look at the sort of freedom that human beings have." [19]

Monitoring and evaluation

The removals of obstructions to freedoms are the broad development objective of the project. This development is delivered by enhancing the agency of each individual within the community to improve his individual life. The success with which the project is able to enhance individual freedoms becomes subject to monitoring and evaluation. If the project has already proposed substantial components of inductive community-led evaluation initiatives then traditional externally led, blue print, deductive evaluation approaches cannot come up with the right answers. We need to go further in our evaluations and accept judgemental conclusions in addition to numerical measurements, to accept interpretative conclusions in addition to descriptive ones. Evaluating the results of a Freedom Approach we must anticipate that there could be variable outcomes that are not pre-determined in the project design and anticipate that the community and its individual households could well be engaged in self-led evaluations that may or may not be easily observable to external evaluators.

Sen has always maintained this is an entirely operation-based approach and that when you apply it to buildings, habitat or planning relief or to a general evaluation of a country's progress or, for that matter, cultural freedom, you will have to deal with the issue of evaluation and you will index. The HDI is one way of doing this.

According to Desai the HDI is important because it provide indicators. It is a measure and not an explanation. It asks you to reprioritize what is important and in terms of GNP, the HDI has actually stood up because

Mehbub ul Haq was right. Desai believes that unless you can explain the HDI on a street corner to someone who is not a development consultant or economist, then it will not have meaning and will be misunderstood. "In creating the Human Development Index it was the first time people were able to tell stories that referred to the goals of human development in contrast to GNP. The idea that there should be a Removing Unfreedoms approach offers the same value. You will never find all the different things that need to be done, things to enhance. That is not necessary. What it will do is to spur thinking and then action." [20]

The Human Development Index

When Mahbub ul Haq asked Sen to design the HDI some 15 years ago Sen had great reservations and explained to us, at the LSE colloquium, how he advised Haq that it was naive to believe that one number could represent all human development. Sen went so far as to say it was vulgar. In the end he explained it was a very hard thing to do and he did it with great complaint. According to Sen, Haq always insisted that even if you get international acceptance of the human development approach, you will not get people using it as they do the GDP or GNP unless you have one number. Haq argued that even if it is vulgar, you have to use it. However it would be a different purpose to argue for human development at a general level, as human development is not dependent on the HDI, not even in terms of measurement. Sen demonstrated there is a lot of confusion about what constitutes a measure. He explained you get 60 different numbers that form the measure. It is a vector measure. And it can be used in a standard fashion. For example when we say it was a very unpleasant day, by which we mean it's hot and humid and we can add some other factors, like there was no breeze and so on. If someone were to ask you to 'convert that into one index' Sen explains, it would be a silly way of going about it. He would argue it is a question of having basic components there. 'Similarly all the tables of human development are given different features which are important so one has to stand up for that, rather than decry HDI.'

Source: LSE Colloquium 7 July 2003

Amartya Sen and the Asian Alliance

The Removing Unfreedoms research project was carried out over a three-year period. During that time these ideas were discussed with urban development consultants and discussions were recorded between all the participants. The results of these discussions can be accessed on the website www.removingunfreedoms.org. Central to these efforts was a workshop in Mumbai, India, with NSDF, the Mahila Milan Women's Savings Group and the NGO, SPARC, which supports their concerns. This location was suggested by DFID, which has an ongoing programme with SPARC. We were welcomed by SPARC who were willing to work with us and consider the potentials of the Freedom Approach for their project with the slums dwellers. Anticipating the requirements of the workshop with them, we let our inquiry be guided by discussions with Rick Davies, a professional evaluator based in the UK, who edits Monitoring and Evaluations News – a publication supported by numerous international NGOs.

The Freedom Approach and workshop objectives

The extent of our interaction with the NSDF and SPARC was limited by time. We were not there to carry out a measured evaluation. We simply intended to hold intense discussions with the NGO to try and determine whether in their work they could find any relevance in the Freedom Approach and if a common urban development framework based on freedoms could be community led and shared locally by all actors including the community, other NGO's and international donors, agencies and institutions.

In particular we wanted to discover whether the community of slum dwellers accepted the idea of the individual as an agent of change and whether it was possible for an individual to express in any way his or her ideas about the things they value. Rick Davies had advised us to interact primarily with SPARC since they are the NGO who has designed the project and who present it to donors. In determining to what extent the individual was the agent of change, he suggested it would be necessary to identify whether individual social decision making was monitored and recorded by SPARC and presented to donors.

Dharavai, Mumbai, India.

All workshop participants agreed to a simple work process to be followed day-to-day. Every morning we were to meet slum dwellers who were facing different obstructions at different locations. The groups including the Mahila Milan Women's Savings Group, at Byculla; the resettlement residents of the Urban Transport Project, Mankhurd, Transit Camp; the Residents of Rajiv Indira Housing Block, Dharavi; and the community who run the Mumbai toilet construction projects. We would also join the savings collection of the pavement dweller collective. In the afternoon we would meet for ongoing discussion sessions with the administrators of SPARC.

We established at the start that we were going to have problems explaining the term 'freedoms'. Freedom is associated with India's 'Freedom Struggle' led by Gandhi. In our discussions, the process of gaining freedoms was therefore explained as a process of removing obstructions or constraints in the lives of the slum dwellers. We linked our observations from these dialogues, to four stages of a project cycle. Anyone designing a project based on the Freedom Approach could take these observations into consideration at the project design stage.

Project cycle

Defining the context

When considering the context of the NSDF project neither SPARC nor the NSDF think in terms of dividing all their obstructions into the five categories of Amartya Sen's freedoms. However the obstructions that Sen mentions – to political freedoms, economic facilities, social opportunities, transparency guarantees and protective security – are most certainly experienced by the slum dwellers as their major obstruction – for example,

Dharavai, Mumbai, India.

finance, housing, healthcare and education, emergency floods and fires, access to information to name a few. The context defined by the NSDF is the provision of 'housing and infrastructure through building the capacity of people's organizations to negotiate their entitlements with governmental, municipal and other public institutions'. The primary constraint to overcome is seen to be security of dwellings rather than an equally weighted list of obstructions spread across the freedom spectrum.

SPARC was established in 1984 at a time when the homes of pavement and railway families were regularly demolished by the Municipal Corporation of Greater Mumbai and traditional NGOs were unable to respond to such crises. At this time the membership of the NSDF was predominately male. When SPARC and NSDF came together one product of their union was the Mahila Milan, which translates as Women Together in English. They formed a network of decentralized savings and credit groups managed by women slum dwellers. The significant addition of the Mahila Milan savings group to the NSDF addressed the socio-political context of the NSDF across India, which had previously not been accepting of the existing knowledge base and skill of the women slum dwellers. SPARC identified a macro-level obstruction blanketed across the entire female population of the slum dwellers in India. While SPARC and NSDF have worked towards supporting a collective participation process and community identity in order to interact with the municipalities and governing authorities, the Mahila Milan Women's Savings Group generates self-management capacities and skills based on the potential and capabilities of each individual.

Identifying the problem and designing the project.

According to Celine D'Cruz, a SPARC administrator, issues of health, education, counselling, and sponsorship were considered in the beginning of their discussions with the NSDF. However every time the subject of demolitions came up it overpowered everything else. Without a fixed address the slum dwellers would not get rations cards, the children would lose their books for school, everything related back to security of tenure. Thus the priority to address the immediate concerns of housing over rode the considerations of other issues. However, to say that the project design has sighted its objectives solely on security of tenure simplifies an extensive umbrella operation that links the mechanism of micro-savings to gender issues and a broad interactive community participation process. The objectives clearly included empowering the individual capability of the slums dwellers to lead they life they value leading.

In designing the project SPARC and the NSDF have made a distinction between the micro-obstructions that effect each member of the community in different ways and the macro-obstructions shared by the community as a whole. The project is designed around two components. The first is the Mahila Milan Women's Savings Group that has evolved through an analysis of the relationships discovered in the families of slum dwellers. They share Sen's advice in working to discover the issues previously overlooked. Rather than question 'why can't the slum dwellers put savings aside to invest in a future home?' they asked, 'Who in the family has the stronger incentive to save?' The results identified how women in extreme economic crisis have a stronger potential to save money than their husbands. Therefore by designing in an objective for a Mahila Milan Women's Savings Group, SPARC could strengthen and support the women's potential to manage their finances. There is no doubting the success of the Mahila Milan Savings Group. However, for Sen, the approach would need to go one step further with this reasoning and identify the capability of the women as an objective in itself. Once that is established you can then identify the capability to achieve economic security and land tenure. From a freedom perspective there are two separate issues here but in many ways the implementation of the Mahila Milan Women's Savings Groups addresses this concern.

The second component for NSDF is the formation of Collective Federations. The design of the collective aims to achieve a decentralized participation process that will successfully target a wider and more sustained level of self-governance and citizenship while reducing the communities' dependence upon the state or municipality. The participating process begins with the Mahila Milan Women's Savings Group but scales up to become a collective. The collectives form federations to be mobilized as an instrument for interaction with the authorities. The presence of a collective ensures serious consideration from the authorities and exerts a pressure that is not so much for removing all general macro-obstructions but specifically for securing land, building rights and transit housing facilities for families who have been forced out from slum locations. In doing so, other priorities to do with ration cards, toilets and sanitation, water and electricity accessibility, have likewise received a profiled recognition by the municipality. In transit camps, ration shops have been set up to distribute kerosene and other commodities and the slum dwellers names on the electoral rolls are transferred to the relocation settlements. SPARC and NSDF have pushed to the forefront issues of citizenship, politics and self-governance as the leading dialogue in their interaction with the municipality

According to Sen, a development approach is measured by the success in moving the entire community forward. He describes this process as ever-expanding freedoms implying that once urban development policies engage with a Freedom Approach, the design objectives become part of a continuum and will necessarily expand their activities to the next stage as a matter of course. As Desai said there is no stop to democracy.

For SPARC and the NSDF a case in point is the 'Community-Led Infrastructure Finance Facility' (CLIFF), a more recent addition to their design objective. CLIFF has emerged directly out of their experience with providing housing and the difficulties in securing medium and large-scale loan guarantees. SPARC is a trust and trusts have difficulties in borrowing money to manage their assets. Sheela Patel, the director of SPARC, explained that they could only go so far in supporting the physical infrastructure necessary for large-scale relocation of the slum dwellers. "There is

Transit camp, Mumbai, India.

a substantial additional risk in their work that brings very complex guarantee arrangements. Thousands and millions could be spent doing projects that would just fall by the wayside because of the inability to get a loan guarantee at the scaling up stage. SPARC has demonstrated for over 25 years how they have expanded microfinance facilities to construct the necessary social and physical infrastructure essential for NSDF. NSDF is an enterprising federation and not a rent seeking institution. However, in scaling up the community-based project, the financial security gap becomes most apparent. Some sort of state, municipal, regional and or bridging finance is required. We needed someone to give a venture capital and say, okay, take this—it is yours and show us what you can do."[21]

Through dialogue with DFID, Homeless International and Cities Alliance, CLIFF is now a piloted project in Mumbai with the NSDF. Start-up financing of £7 million has been provided and the Swedish Government has also made a commitment to provide an additional US$2 million to support the initiative. The financial assistance is designed to act as a non-refundable bridging loan to take on and share the NSDF risks, including advising on risk management and assisting in their strategy to support community-initiated housing and infrastructure construction projects. CLIFF provides the developmental freedom that has been generated from the individual and collective action of NSDF and SPARC. In considering what the most appropriate solution to this immediate situation is, the objective agreed is to increase the slum dwellers access to commercial and public sector finance, the absence of which has remained a major obstruction to the project's progress. CLIFF will provide the economic security and assist the NSDF to become their own developers in partnership with local municipalities.

Planning and implementation

Implementing the activities of both the Mahila Milan Women's Savings Group and the collective federations includes initiating actions at the micro (individual) level as well as at the macro (community) level as suggested in the Freedom Approach. The design of the implementation process has been very specific to the community of slum dwellers and no one has forced the women or the households to join the savings group and save money. On the contrary, its success relies on the determination of the individual participating in the process. The implementation of the project has been decided as an outcome of participation and re-ordering of needs. Even so, according to Sen's Freedom Approach, the macro priority should remain flexible as the value attached may change. For example, the immediate threat of demolitions confronting the slum dwellers must be addressed as a priority and linked to the long-term infrastructure goal of attaining tenure. Both must be reocgnized as a process by the municipalities. recognized as a process by the municipalities. At the same time these objectives are identified, the broader macro concerns will establish a process that can re-evaluate the criteria by which values are attached to further unfreedoms, the constraints at the individual level that obstruct the capability to lead the life they value living. In this way a constant set of new objectives and activities will be formulated through ongoing discussions and participation with citizens.

The Mahila Milan Women's Saving Group

The Mahila Milan's activities include collecting savings from the woman of the household every day. The long-term priority is to provide housing. Daily collections encourage the discipline of saving and the management of funds from her daily household expenses. Each household has a savings book in which the daily savings are recorded and maintained by the collector. Importantly the majority of the families participating in the women's

Mahila Milan members, Mumbai, India.

saving group are illiterate and the communication with the daily savings collector places a higher value on verbal communication and memory than on written documents. The only written documentation identifies the amount of money collected from each household. Individual or family difficulties are often made apparent if the daily saving becomes irregular in anyway. Individual social concerns or grievances take the form of spoken discussions that are memorized including details spanning the livelihoods of the 50 households. Each evening the saving collectors meet to review the savings pulse of the whole community and identify any difficulties and grievances among the households. Communicating the information takes place through the telling of individual stories. In this manner individual concerns and obstructions are brought to the attention of the federation and collective decisions agree the best method to remove the obstructions.

For example, in the case of one husband's death, the federation decided to give funds to the widow so she could continue with her work as a collector for the Mahila Milan and support her children. When another woman's husband was arrested, again funds were made available to assist her. In the case of emergencies such as fire or floods, the individuals involved would be brought to the attention of the federation and funds would become available to assist. Extended families can include grandparents and sons and daughters-in-law living in the same house. In a case where a mother and daughter relationship became polarized the federation would address the issue and attempt mediation and propose alternative solutions. If an individual or family needed immediate access to their saving funds because of a crisis, these are made available even in the middle of the night.

Once the household establishes their saving process, the Mahila Milan women agree that the first priority for most women is to purchase kitchen equipment. The second priority is assisting their husbands in finding work. They then will prioritize education, health and so on accordingly. Remarkably the saving group process allows for the micro individual concerns to be addresses while the collective focus remains geared to interchanges with the municipality on issues of housing, demolitions and relocations.

The key activity in implementing the entire development mechanism of the NSDF and Mahila Milan participation process is communication and yet no details are written down aside from the savings figures in rupees.

The entire development strategy, implementation and replication process relies on oral spoken traditions including memory facilities and spontaneous arrangements.

The women clearly have their own culture and speak with conviction, intelligence and humanity with regard to life they want to lead. Sheela Patel, the Director of SPARC, goes to great lengths to defend the energy and spirit of the Mahila Milan women and to share their hardships and success stories personally with women in other cities globally. Key to their success is their voice and their generosity of time and experience. This explains why SPARC and the NSDF are at a loss to document the interaction and rely on physically taking evaluators, ourselves included, to the women's meeting to experience their method first hand.

Women are regarded as having a natural facility to talk and share experiences and concerns. This could also account for the personal attention they are able to give to households when collecting savings. It is remarkable that even when the women have not yet

Pavement dwellers. Mumbai, India.

Mahila Milan. Receiving payment, Mumbai, India.

Mahila Milan. Recording payment, Mumbai, India.

acquired a home after 15 years of savings – as it may take that long – they still believe in the process and share a sense of patience and perseverance which has inspired a savings group methodology replicated and working in 50 cities across India and in 11 countries.

Collective particpation methodology

SPARC and the NSDF have created an equally unique methodology to address the macro-objective of supporting slum dwellers to create a collective community identity based on shared concerns. The collective identity addresses evictions, resettlement and housing issues as its primary goal. In the case of demolitions the individuals can be mobilized as a collective to take responsibility for the demolition of their own home. This allows them to be in control and know that their personal belongings are saved and not destroyed each time. The participation process produces intense responses between the members. From the start, as soon as a savings group settlement is identified as an area, its initial representation begins on the basis of one leader for 50 households or one representative for 100 households to collect savings. These representatives attend the sub-federation meetings. Then the sub-federations elect their representatives. The representation mechanism is based on their commitment and accountability as voluntary saving managers to those people from whom they collect savings and whom they represent the Federation at meetings.

Membership

If a group of slum dwellers want to become members, initially they must demonstrate they can function as a collective and gain the agreement of most of the people in their settlement to take part in the daily saving process. If more than 50 per cent of the people in their settlement are interested then their standing can be recognized as a collective. When SPARC and NSDF are convinced that a particular community is ready to join the federation they check whether the new committee is in a city with an existing federation, or in a new area. Regardless of where they are in India, somebody from the national committee and a representative from the local area will go to visit the new community and explain the process of how they start a savings scheme, including how to begin collecting information and determining priorities.

Training

If slum dwellers want to become members but do not understand the process, then SPARC offers them the opportunity to attend a five day training session with an existing saving group in order to experience what the federations are doing. In this way they experience the idea of how it works by hearing other personal experiences, seeing the process in action and observing how members engage with each other. The prospective members can visualize where the process might lead several years down the line. Giving people a real image is enough for them to make a membership decision, according to Patek, because they already know what their obstructions are and have prioritized issues of land, housing, water and so on. SPARC and NSDF will then advise them to meet with a federation who shares the same needs in negotiating land, water or whatever the feature priority may be. The new members are observed through further exchanges, discussions and then SPARC and NSDF reviews the new group's commitment over time.

Community-led evaluations

Within the established federations there is a strong political commitment to assessing who owns the knowledge. Surveys are designed to the criteria of what is considered acceptable to the community. A survey based on criteria not established by the people will not go very far in representing the capabilities of the slum dwellers. For example, take an NGO who wants to do a digitization of all the slums maps in Puna. They may get the sophisticated computer software and hire community members to do the survey. Yet the NGO, in this case, are the ones who do the whole utilization and they own the property not the slum dwellers. On the other hand, if a survey is designed and acceptable to the people, the information will be more accurate and representative of their needs. There is no benefit in a survey that probes subjects that the community does not want to talk about. There is an acceptance that a poor person will not want to divulge certain types of information. According to Sheela Patel, each person should feel comfortable when asking all the questions and stand by the responses everyone gives. The design of the survey takes the form of a public discussion and then that data is collated.

The survey must ask about things that are related to what the slum dwellers prioritize. The object is to produce a database that you can swear by and over a period of time it will become standardized. The collation of the data is first done manually at the location. The people have learned to quantify information. Tomorrow, if they want to provide a small survey they can do it themselves by initiating a public discussion at a specified location. If someone identifies there are altogether 600 households, then the answers can be disaggregated so that 200 households have a particular characteristic, 300 are households do not have a male member and 100 households have so many children. These characteristics are all quantified so that if the people want to go to the municipality they can now provide a quantitative survey and substantiate the specific problems. This process establishes a community-led survey in which the people themselves collate the representations and establish their priorities justified on this information.

SPARC can then arrive at a more sophisticated level of evaluation when this data is put into a database, to then produce a more elaborate report. However the motivation for these reports is based on the external demands of donors, as it is not useful for the slum dwellers. Even so this process, according to Sheela Patel, allows for the most refined sourcing of data and has challenged everything the World Bank has suggested for integration strategies of the slum dwellers. Their process has actually produced a new survey framework.

Leadership

A long standing Mahila Milan representative may spend 50 per cent of her time travelling outside the city, speaking on behalf of the NSDF to other communities, but there are reserve lines of other women to take her place while she is away. When she returns to Mumbai she goes back to her job collecting savings from her 50 households. Becoming a leader or representatives does not stop the women from continuing with their role as collector in the daily savings community. For Patel this is the important dynamic of leadership which maintains the quality of direct participation in the development process. An example is Jockin, the president of the NSDF, who is very involved in day-to-day activities of arbitration discourse and in the decision-making between NSDF and SPARC. Responsibility is not deferred to a purely professional person. Critical choices in the day-by-day activities are still made by all the administrators because only by continuing in that participation can you address all the other deeper dimensions and political issues that exist. This process advances a more mature, long-term quality of leadership. In many ways this process assumes an in-built sense of continuity.

Structure

SPARC has structured its relationship with the NSDF in the form of collectives and federations, as thousands of slum dweller households are dispersed in different settlement areas across the city. Below the city level they have created sub-federations. The sub-federations are not defined by geography but by principality and landowner, because the active participation foundation dialogue is with the landowner who owns the land on which the people have settled. A federation comes into existence where the critical mass is substantial enough to merit this identification. Each location has particular problems. SPARC's long-term dream is presently realized in one respect by the Railway Slum Dwellers Federation. The problems experienced on the railway land are replicated all over the country and all over the world. According to Patel 'if you go to Manila, South Africa or to any country, there is land along the railway track being encroached by human settlements and this produces numerous settlements with no organisation or identity.' Through the implementing of a savings group participation process, NSDF and SPARC have initiated dialogues to generate community identities based on the specific characteristics facing the community. The Railway Slum Dwellers Federations can communicate with other railway federations across the country or in the different parts of the world. This is a primary example of how a successful Freedom Approach to development can be scaled up to national and international levels.

Administration

Initially, the committee is made up by people who are willing to volunteer their time. In this role they must be willing to attend periodic five-day session and observe how the savings groups operate in the different locations. In 2003 there were 72 representatives from 38 cities that had established sufficiently sustained and successful collectives to warrant a representative. These representatives sub-divide themselves on a state level and then a northern and southern level. From these divisions they conduct regional meetings and state-level meetings. There are 15 to 20 people who form part of the core team with Jockin and work full time for the federations. They receive an honorarium daily rate. These 'core team' representatives accompany the slum dwellers and become the link between the federations, reporting to SPARC who assists in setting up plans, writing proposals for specific projects or acting as intermediaries to negotiate with the state, financial institutions and principalities. By and large the management of the federations' growth is addressed by NSDF. As the infrastructure and participation process has matured, SPARC has shed and abdicated many more organizational responsibilities to the communities within the federations and has hired consultants who will take up the specific technical issues, such as like architects and engineers. SPARC's long-term overall growth plans are not to expand to every city but to maintain a core team in Mumbai.

Monitoring, evaluation and assessing the impact

The first monitoring and evaluation of individual social concerns takes place with the women's saving group. The evaluation takes place daily during the collection of payments. The amount of savings collected is recorded and there is no other written documentation of any evaluations or arrangements between the individual slum dwelling families. All arrangements regarding individual social choice are identified and discussed within the oral culture domain of NSDF and SPARC. SPARC protects this undocumented area of interchange within the NSDF from intrusions of external evaluations. They feel community-led evaluations are the only way to make observable the inductive, multi-layered analysis of the illiterate slum dwellers.

SPARC has supported the NSDF in initiating community-led surveys that identify numbers of households and quantitative information that can be used within the municipality and for donors and international agencies. Some of these processes are extremely innovative and have gained attention from international institutions including the World Bank. However, when we applied the criteria of a Freedom Approach to the monitoring of individual social choice, as observed within the remarkable social arrangements utilized by the Mahila Milan Women's Savings Group, it became clear that these human development successes are not made observable to donors, other NGOs or international agencies. In other words, the community-led development process that takes places in the oral spoken domain is not recorded, documented, monitored or evaluated in terms of the ability of each person to take part in social choice activities that provide the options necessary to lead the life they value living. The full impact of these observations are explored in the section: Monitoring social decision making.

The greatest potential for change

The NSDF represent the middle city inhabitants who rely on an alternative culture of spoken words and memory capabilities. Their community is often dictated by more spontaneous activities. We have seen how these citizens have the greatest obstructions and therefore the greatest potential for initiating change. However, what tends to happen in the normal process of governments in India and in most countries, is the macro, written culture seeks to dominate the oral culture. In other words it regards the oral culture as the underdeveloped form of society. These are the circumstances in which we have to ask what in our society is considered knowledge? To a larger extent the kind of knowledge valued in the written culture was defined in the nineteenth century society, that to be literate is to be advanced. Somehow there is always the pressure that the urban culture of the slum dwellers must be formalized and enter the domain of the written culture as an institution.

The interchange between these two urban cultures is one of the oldest partnerships in all major urban environments where both are needed. In many ways the dynamic of city is bound by the complexity of the interchange of this relationship. Urban policy makers and planners speak of social patterns and urban economies and yet the relationship between the macro-urban cultures and the middle city inhabitants remains unrealized. SPARC's role acts as a buffer for the slum dwellers and illustrates the potential for an NGO to mediate between the two worlds. In a sense SPARC tells the authorities, the donors and international agencies that there is nothing for you beyond here that will make any sense to your expectations. The kind of information you require and all the aspects by which you organize your authority, transfer knowledge and communicate to other institutions is not necessary for our process with the slum dwellers. Within the accepted methodologies SPARC has translated the necessary information for the donors, agencies and institutions as effectively as possible. Beyond this translation, as of yet there is nothing the authorities, donors or institutions will be able to interpret with any accuracy.

According to Sheela Patel, there is a deep discomfort and suspicion from both sides of the monitoring and evaluation process. There is a crisis in trying to communicate with the evaluators. On the one hand we experience their human face and at the same time their remote methodologies. "We are faced with their criteria and their inability to envision what we are doing. They are blocked by the sense of comfort in their structures and frameworks that they already have produced which makes a complete distortion of what we say and what we discuss."[21]

Clearly SPARC and NSDF, whether they realize it or not, have directed their efforts to working with Sen's ideas of social choice theory and individual social agency. And yet both the criteria of measuring freedom – that would make observable their successes – and the qualitative evaluations – and information base necessary for monitoring purposes – do not yet exist.

Monitoring social decision making

During the workshop in Mumbai, the process of social decision making within the Mahila Milan Women's Savings Group and the NSDF through to SPARC was identified. SPARC's interface with donors and national agencies was then documented. Using a diagram on a flip chart we could distinguish different levels of actors and communication in the monitoring and evaluations process.

The first level identified the written domain of communication dominated by objective, deductive evaluation and reporting. This is the domain primarily used by external evaluators to other NGOs, donors and international government agencies.

The second level identified the role of SPARC who provides the necessary interface between the macro-urban culture and the middle city inhabitants of NSDF. SPARC supports the NSDF in initiating development change and in the process documents all their activities and makes them legitimate in the face of authorities and government institutions. In their role as a supporting organization SPARC, is aware of the possible unfavourable or inaccurate conclusions and consequences of objective external evaluations. SPARC takes on the responsibility of accessing the inductive self-evaluations of the community and translating it into data for the external evaluations of other NGO's, donors and government agencies. SPARC argues that community-led evaluations are the only way social decision arrangements could address the inductive multi-layered analysis of the oral domain.

The third level represents the representatives of the NSDF who receive the daily honorarium and work full time for the NSDF. They are the ones representing NSDF concerns in arbitration with the municipality, housing infrastructure, finance, mobilizing the collectives and monitoring the

Urban Development Communication and Community-led Evaluation

Monitoring individual social decision-making at the local level

Macro Urban Culture Written Domain	First Level ↑	National and International: Donors Agencies Institutions
	Second Level ↑　　↑	NGO: SPARC
Middle City Culture Oral Domain	Third Level ↑　↑　↑	Representatives: NSDF
	Fourth Level ↑ ↑ ↑ ↑ ↑ ↑ ↑ ↑	Individual Agents of Change: Women's Savings Group Slum Dwellers

The Mahila Milan Women's savings collectors visit each household every day and are in a position to discuss and monitor the obstructions. From this step a community-led evaluation process would be decided from within the community through exposure to discussions that identify the issues at the individual household level. Together the community would establish legitimacy and transparency and identify the success and obstructions of individual agency within the Freedom framework and so convert the oral culture into something that can be communicated to donors, governments and agencies.

Mahila Milan Women's Savings Groups nationally. This level is distinguished as the first contact with the oral culture of the slum dwellers. The absence of written data is indicative of communities that are not literate. Oral agreements and arrangements are the means by which social decisions are identified and by which arrangements are achieved.

The fourth level is the slum dwellers themselves and the Mahila Milan Women Savings Group. The oral domain of the Mahila Milan is based on inductive, subjective evaluations and reporting by the saving collectors to the community. A multitude of skills and assets have been acquired that have proved necessary for the step-by-step process to transform their situation. As Mahila Milan Women's Saving Group operates solely in the oral domain, the many successes of their innovative method of development, although protected by SPARC, is at present not made observable, or evaluated to a wider shared audience in the upper levels of the communication diagram.

More work could be done that would establish and enable the slum dwellers to lead their own evaluations and list their own obstructions. An NGO, like SPARC, could rearrange these into five or more categories outlined by Sen in order to communicate the success or failure in removing unfreedoms to the public institutions. If citizens could begin to evaluate their own success, the successes being the degree to which the obstructions and constraints to their freedoms have been removed, then we can ensure that the process of development expands their ability to lead the life they value leading.

A new breakthrough could be achieved in formulating a common framework that would make observable the successes through a multi-objective Freedom Framework. The framework could be shared vertically between slum dwellers and also horizontally across the federations of slum dwellers in different parts of the world, between NGO's and public and government institutions. Table 3 illustrates the policy implications of the freedom-centred approach and gives a bird eye view of the issues outlined in this book. The obstructions facing the lives of the NSDF are included. While admittedly it is an over simplification of the complexity of the issues we have discussed, it does provide an overview and guide for opportunities to enlarge urban policy frameworks that can be shared by both communities and donors.

Conclusion

The planning and operational success of SPARC and NSDF can advise urban policy makers with a deeper understanding of participatory development process for cities today. Currently SPARC and NSDF have now set up a Section 25, not for profit, company. The idea of a project is generated within the Federation and SPARC. All the construction business that the federation produces is negotiated for by SPARC, Mahila Milan and NSDF and contracted through the company to execute, as they have raised the equity through CLIFF. They are now in a position to negotiate with Mumbai Metropolitan Regional Development Authority (MMRDA) and to be the lead organisation in the design and re-location of 35,000 to 45,000 households who MMRDA requires to be relocated for various projects.

The entire relocation project takes place through the MMRDA under the Slum Rehabilitation Act. They give the land and the right to get the money back. It is a new concept in Mumbai. MMRDA will identify the end users and SPARC will work with MMRDA to do the relocation work based on their experience with the NSDF

The scale of these projects required a tendering process and SPARC and NSDF lobbied for a tender document that gave an equal playing field to SPARC as the NGO organization representing the NSDF communities. The NSDF quality of intervention has legitimate recognition but they were unable to satisfy the tendering requirement to be registered with MMRDA. They had to establish an alternative and have it recognized officially. When the tender came out SPARC applied on behalf of the federations. All the tender fees, paid like guarantees, were taken care of by CLIFF. The implications for the NSDF communities are impressive. In the past the contractor who received the contract would go ahead and construct the building without any contact with or knowledge of the relocation populations. Typically these contracts consider the physical work as the primary objective and relocation concerns secondary. SPARC has created a precedent in the process of this building project. The primary objective is in negotiating and fulfilling the obligations of relocating people and the physical work is secondary. These are very important issues for the people. Therefore SPARC and NSDF have set a model for urban development policy that will transform the way the relocation of slum dwellers is implemented in the city.

Restoring and sustaining cultural diversity

In terms of a Freedom Approach, this project now presents very interesting development opportunities as it entails 1700 homes, or almost 15,000 people. There is the possibility to reconsider the administration of the area in terms of opting out of the municipal system for certain services and governance. The municipality can obstruct very significant community achievements and potentials. The building bylaws are one example as they are so severe and geared towards a certain type of habitation. They lay out certain rules specifying how much you can build, what schools you must have, etc.. All these restrictions can be reconsidered if 17,000 people are relocated at one time.

If we compare the building byelaws in non-residential area to that of residential area – which has a finite object like a house on it – the nature of the habitat obstructions are more evident. The residential byelaws restrict what you can do to a house over the course of time and do not anticipate events that might prove to be determining factors to family needs in regard to changing social, cultural, ecological or even political events. On the other hand, non-residential area byelaws lay down that you cannot build on lands, even lands encroached on by thousands of slum dwellers settlements. The slum dwellers, as an urban culture, have different values and requirements. Their needs may entail a different sort of shelter with a host of other features that would be decided by the community through discussions.

These concerns refer back to fundamental issues concerning Sen's Freedom Approach to urban policy and the formation of mega-cities. Sen believes if we continue with traditional planning regulations we will not address the real causes underlying slums and poverty. We have observed how urbanization ideals and byelaws result from assumptions within dominant written cultures and have restricted planning and buildings to certain types of habitations that prescribe a kind of organization of space and habitats through regulations. They do not always reflect the values or lifestyles of all the people and can create obstructions to the communities' capability to function effectively. These laws are set in place without conferring with the communities and do not consider alternative opportunities required by the growing diversity of migrant cultures.

With a relocation of 17,000 people SPARC and the NSDF have the opportunity to question the process regarding administration of the municipality and the whole question of the municipal taxation. There is an opportunity to ask how to negotiate and inform the municipality in regard to certain community-led initiatives that are going to change the way we need to live. First they could discuss what is the taxation structure? The NSDF would provide a governance system that would work and if it did not and if there were any problems the municipality could take over. By taking this opportunity and establishing these discussions thorough the NSDF there is an opportunity for urban policy makers to re-evaluate the priorities of good urban governance. The further away from the front door you can keep the municipality, the greater is the community participation in what is actually the most important role of local civil governance. This could be the next objective SPARC and NSDF undertake.

Table 3: Summary Policy Framework: a wider approach to foster development

INSTRUMENTS Constituents of a person's freedom that enhance his capabilities and potentials to live a life he values.	ARRANGEMENTS Rights, opportunities and entitlements that enable expansion of human development and freedom.	CONSTRAINTS on the enhancement of a person's potentials and capabilities – Types of unfreedoms	EVALUATIONS Assessments required to inform policy makers about capabilities and potentials of development		SOME EXISTING STRATEGIES And policy goals compared to the wider, ever-enhancing goals of development as a freedom from constraints.	
			on the technocratic, top-down, quantitative side	on the democratic, bottom-up, qualitative, subjective side	The Habitat Agenda	DFID Urban Strategy Paper 2000
POLITICAL FREEDOM	Institutional arrangements. Forums for free debate. Ability to participate in public discussions. Protection for dissenters. Free media. Existence of political parties. Elected bodies. Facilities to scrutinize authorities. Constitutional arrangements to ensure checks and balances between judiciary, legislature and executive. Decentralization. Citizen's participation.	Absence of civil rights Denial of political liberty Press-censorship Presence of undue influence to constrict market mechanisms Absence of critical public discussion Authoritarian rule Absence of access to telecommunication Political manipulation by vested interests	Persons imprisoned. Voting rights. Access to written, electronic and broadcast media. Access to libraries. Women in government, police, etc. Access to telecommunication.	Constraints to voting. Access to voting booths. Constraints on legal access. Constraints on access to law and order services. Nature of land title. Constraints on access to information. Constraints to act as representatives. Constraints on use of telecommunications. Whether Constitution or law promotes the right to adequate housing. Whether Constitution includes protections against eviction. Other housing related rights (gender sensitive). Institutional arrangements between central and local governments and balance of power between them.	Decentralization and strengthening of local authorities, association and networks. Popular participation and civic engagement. Participatory and consultative mechanisms. Capacity building and institutional development.	Develop the capacity of local actors to manage pro-poor urban development and regional growth. Strengthen efforts by the international community to support the urbanization process which involves the participation of poor people. Need for governments to provide enabling, legislative and regulatory framework, pro-poor and market sensitive. Empowering poor people themselves to demand and realize their rights and entitlements. Optimize opportunities of decentralization. Support civil society advocates for poor people's needs and political participation.
ECONOMIC FACILITIES	Open labour market. Protection from bondage. Spaces and opportunities for free economic exchange. Access to product markets. Saving opportunities. Stable business ethics. Title to land. Freedom for women to seek employment outside home. Access to credit.	No employment opportunities Low income Arbitrary controls on transaction High inflation Indebtedness Labour bondage Market controlled by vested interest Price fixing and manipulation Unfair tradeProhibitions Market monopoly	Male female employment. Income. Earned income share in family. Loans from banks. Youth unemployment rate. Children in employment. Women's GDP per capita.	Percentage of family income retained by women. Loans from money lenders. Interest rate on loans compared to market rate. Individual disabilities. Constraints to mobility. Access to credit. constraints on women to seek employment. Access to training facilities. Access to transport. Access to markets. Recovery of dues.	Financing shelter and human settlements. Gender equality. Improving urban economies. Enabling markets to work. Mobilising sources of finance. Ensuring access to land.	Support to the private sector for PPP; small business and socially responsible business. DFID will work to increase the capacity of cities to attract investment and to develop improved links with rural economies. Need to ensure that the distribution of the opportunities of economic growth reach the poor. Develop the capacity of local actors to manage pro-poor urban development and regional growth.

SOCIAL OPPORTUNITIES	Good health. Basic education. Encouragement and cultivation of initiatives. Gender equity. Women's well being. Child care. Property rights for women.	Under nutrition. Premature mortality. Absences of services. Gender exploitation. Low income. Illiteracy. Child labour. High child mortality. Lack of hospital services. Lack of nutrition supplements. Selective property rights. Low female literacy. Urban violence.	Life expectancy. Birth and death rates. Contraception rates. Infant mortality. Maternal mortality. Infant immunization. Access to health services. Access to safe water. Access to sanitation. Birth attended by health personal. Population per doctor. Underweight babies. Malnourished children. Calorie intake. Adult literacy. Mean years of schooling. Primary enrolment.	Access to alternative medicine practitioners. Access to fuel. Stability of dwelling. Domestic injuries. Exposure to pollution. Constraints on water access. Constraints on school attendance. School drop out rate. Unattended children. Working children under 10. Children per class. Children per teacher. Distance from primary school. Areas considered dangerous or inaccessible to police.	Need for economic development, social development and environ-mental protection. Ensuring access to basic infrastructure. Environment sustainability. Conservation of historic and cultural heritage.	DFID will contribute to programmes that help to improve the living and working conditions of the poor: water and sanitation; energy sources; tenure arrangements; supply of land for housing and health and safety. Poor people should benefit from improved health care, better education opportunities.
TRANSPARENCY GUARANTEES	Absence of corruption. Mechanisms for seeking justice. Guarantees of disclosures and lucidity. Speedy judicial decisions. Access to police protection.	Corruption. Financial irresponsibility. Protected under-hand dealings. Insecure banking system. Unchallenged governance. Bullying and intimidation by organized 'mafias'. Constraints on access justice and police.		Settlement of transacted work. Time spent on bondage obligations. Facilities to report crime. Presence of women in police station. Unreported thefts. Unreported molestation. Non-formal payments for services, shelter and work. Regular independent auditing of municipal accounts. Published contracts and tenders. Sanctions against faults of civil servants. Laws on disclosure of potential conflicts of interest. Civil society involved in alteration in zoning. Civil society involved in major public projects.	Strengthen shelter-related information system.	Improve DFID's and others' capacities to address the urban challenge through information support, and knowledge and research development. Improve local accountability systems. Need to access and to negotiate information so to negotiate on a more equal footing with others.
PROTECTIVE SECURITY	Network arrangements to mitigate disasters. Emergency facilities for rescue and damage control. Shelters. Subsidy for victims of famine and disasters. Arrangement for protection of extreme deprivation.	Famine. Neglected natural disaster effects. Absence of administrative network.	Catastrophic deaths. Destroyed houses. Destroyed schools and health centres. Epidemic cases. Density of population before and after calamity. Existence of shelters.	Access to communication networks. Access to emergency food-programmes. Duration of migration. Distance of migration. Nature of resettlement. Emergency and delay. Constraints to access shelter.	Disaster prevention, mitigation and post-disaster rehabilitation capabilities.	

- 12 -

National Urban Recovery Programme: Afghanistan

We have discussed earlier the challenge of adopting shared policy frameworks and trying to implement them across a variety of communities. While national governments need to be at the forefront of this implementation, in most cases – and particularly in developing countries or war-torn countries such as Afghanistan – there is lack of technical, financial and human capacity to manage this process, as well as lack of political commitment and will. Other actors, such as international donors and agencies, will have a major role, while NGOs, the private sector and education institutions will have a very limited role. National level institutions in Afghanistan have not represented community interests and participation processes have not been established previously. Nevertheless, the only way a shared policy freedom framework will be effective is through the social commitment and endorsement of the government that such an approach is required for development. All stakeholders would then be required to share and take on board the freedoms objectives.

A partial approach directed solely at micro-levels and collective community activities is only part of the programme and will not be able to address development in a balanced way. Thus the incentive for a comprehensive urban freedom approach will be driven from national-level policy and encourage local communities to become more aware of this complex situation and to use their voice to participate in the development process. Such participatory evaluation will need to determine whether local communities have enough freedom of opportunity to participate and whether the community will share this freedom with the actors who are promoting development.

The issue of inter-donor coordination is equally relevant to the success of the Freedom Approach. As explained earlier, in order to tackle the complexities of underdevelopment, one would need to cast a much wider net than any unilateral aid agency could do on its own. Experience has shown how unilateral donor strategies often strike against the potential role of lead agencies because their own agendas are narrower than those of a lead agency. Therefore an urban recovery programme advocating the social concerns of Sen – tuned to policy and strategic aims – cannot be successfully implemented without the lead of an international agency. As we have explained earlier, a lead agency could hold up the framework through which donors could address their individual concerns in each country. However, if one were to define a simple framework at the lead agent's level, then donors could enter the field through this common framework and submit the results of their initiatives to a common evaluation procedure, thus formulating a shared platform for the evaluation of successes and failures.

This chapter lays out a proposed project cycle for a National Urban Recovery Programme based on the Freedom Approach to development.[22] Building on Sen's ideal of ever-expanding freedoms, the proposal is more a strategy for an ongoing formulation process leading to a master plan for Afghanistan. However there is no predetermined development formula. Rather, through a careful contextual analysis of the current situation, the proposal sets in motion a realistic Development as Freedom Master Plan for the people of Afghanistan.

The programme lays down the methodology and processes required to develop the important cities of Afghanistan through capacity building and social integration of sub-projects. This will lead to city level master plans over a five-year period. Throughout the proposed programme, Sen's five freedoms are identified and positioned. The first phase will begin with the master plan project for Kabul and this is seen as a replicable programme for the recovery of the other cities of Afghanistan.

For the purposes of this book detailed project components, detailed national and city-wide implementation, administration and contractual details are not included, nor does this chapter focus on specific rural and agricultural obstructions and analysis.

The idea of the proposal as presented is to illustrate the outline guiding principles of a Freedom Approach for a national urban recovery programme.

Project cycle: defining the context

Transitional economies

Afghanistan's economy is in transition and is slow in adjusting to the normalization process. Prior to the Taliban regime, the structure of the economy was divided into the sectors required for a centralized Socialist planning system. The subsequent occupation by Taliban forces disrupted the Soviet initiatives and created enormous uncertainty in certain sectors of

Taxis line up in
Kabul city centre,
Afghanistan.

(Karen Robinson/
Panos)

the economy, particularly those relating to public administration and to the pivotal role that cities needed to play as a stable hub for the Afghan economy. In addition, there are enormous problems with the budgetary deficit that will continue to burden the Afghan economy. While the restructuring of the economic system has proceeded at an uneven pace, political events and inter-community factional fighting continues to unsettle a government caught between the old, relatively isolated ways and a new globally linked system.

International considerations

The future economic and political status of Afghanistan is influenced by its geographical location. It is part of the group of Central Asian countries as well as a potential economic partner of Iran, Pakistan and India. These are the countries that are contiguous to it and could directly support the economy of Afghanistan. Afghanistan needs to adopt tailored strategies to help play a participatory role in the economic markets of the surrounding region. Thus, while adjusting to a new economic relationship with the global economy, Afghanistan must, at the same time, reorient its trade toward its surrounding region in order to generate the surpluses required for economic growth. The cities of Kabul, Kandhahar and Herat will play a major role in these economic re-alignments, as they will provide the hub for channelling investments as well as becoming the nerve centres for communication and dissemination in the regional divisions of the country. This process of city-led economic revitalization will also help to bring about radical changes in its political sphere and the necessary reforms that will build the internal capacity of a more unified nation. These combined measures will bring Afghanistan closer to the acceptable global criteria.

The adoption of measures to gain eventual access to the global economy through its cities can be carried out through an urban recovery programme aimed at the formation of a strong communication network and economic interdependence between its cities. This urban recovery programme would address the problems of transition in the sectors concerned with the political arena, the economic agenda, as well as the socio-cultural expectations. The potential costs of such a transition could be high for Afghanistan because it is still trying to formulate a clearly defined national, political and economic identity after 25 years of totalitarian rule – first under the Soviet state system, which began in 1978, and subsequently under the Taliban regime. Some of these transitional costs relate to:

- complete collapse of city level infrastructures

- high levels of rural migration to the cities

- rising urban unemployment

- negative economic growth, severely damaged rural economy and a reduced gross domestic product

- deterioration of the economic and social welfare support services for urban and rural families

- lack of productive investment opportunities except in real estate

- rapid growth in foreign debt

- excessively high interest rates.

The symptoms of these conditions including soaring inflation (59 per cent in 1998), a depreciating currency and chronic unemployment. The impact of these conditions aggravates the immediate short-term living conditions of the ordinary citizens of Afghanistan. Further aggravation is caused by the massive redundancies and migrations being forced upon the people by a shrinking, inward-looking economy with a precariously situated agricultural sector. These migrant communities become the middle city inhabitants and face the greatest obstructions to the freedom to lead the lives they value leading. The primary focus of the urban recovery programme is the urgent need to address in the short-term the painful effects of the enormous migration into the cities from the countryside. This has caused unemployment and acute housing shortages. The unemployed need to be supported immediately with the help of short-term measures that will not only give gainful employment, but will also at the same time help create the necessary institutional structures to bring acceptable standards of urban life into the cities.

The establishment of a relatively stable and globally acceptable government in Kabul as well as commitments of foreign aid have enabled the adoption of a new global vision to be articulated. National programmes and the enabling legislations will now need to be put in place. It is anticipated that these measures will accelerate the pace of transposition in the cities as well as in agriculture, energy, transport and regional development and in some areas of its internal market.

Recovering municipalities

A particular interest of the programme is to create stable city-level hubs that will lead economic and institutional reform. The Freedom Approach programme has been designed to tackle aspects of both issues at the local city level, starting with Kabul, which is considered to be closer to the location of the problem.

The brunt of the hardships that are being caused by rapid migration and the absence of adequate employment opportunities have been borne by the municipalities. The municipalities administer the urban areas which have not only been destroyed by wars and factional fighting but which also have virtually no infrastructure in place to serve the migrants who are settling there. Enhancing municipal capacity to deal with the problems of urban chaos without creating more unfreedoms for the migrant communities assumes urgency. Evaluations for capacity support by a wide range of aid agencies, as well as the host of NGOs already working in the field, is a means to determine the need for such support.

Aid funds have begun to flow into those institutional arrangements that demonstrate their capacity to implement programmes and projects in support of the city revitalization. It is significant that the most important sources of funds for the immediate development of Afghanistan originate from the West and will be destined for relief-driven programmes and projects.

The role of culture

While at one level Afghanistan is preparing to plan a global role in the future; it is also actively searching for and formulating its unique national identity in the region. Much of its national cultural identity is symbolized by its built heritage. Each municipality has a unique heritage of the built environment as represented by religious monuments, historical buildings and architectural ensembles. Defining the links between the cultural and historical events of the past and the present characteristics of the nation is part of forming the national identity of Afghanistan. With the growing trends towards decentralization, each municipality needs to begin to define its own uniqueness in terms of its special cultural characteristics, events and its built heritage.

This built heritage is in urgent need of revitalization because of years of neglect and lack of maintenance. The revitalization and protection of this built heritage will inevitably assist the process of cultural identification and foster a feeling of optimism amongst the citizens. The built heritage is also the most important tourism asset of each city and its revitalization will therefore form an important component of any tourism revival strategies.

Reviving tourist traffic in the various municipalities of Afghanistan is one of the quickest ways to obtain economic revival. Since much of the basic tourist infrastructure has been damaged, there is a need to recreate modern tourism facilities to cater to a much higher level of demand than currently exists.

Current international assistance objectives

The national interim government has defined Afghanistan's development requirements. They have called for US$45 billion to rebuild the country; the World Bank has estimated that it will cost US$16 billion to rebuild the economy over the next 10 years. In response to these appeals, donors have pledged to provide US$5 billion by July 2004. In a country where the per capita income is estimated to be US$200, the urgent need for reconstruction cannot be exaggerated.

The Removing Unfreedoms Urban Recovery Programme (REMDP) suggests three proposed projects that will form part of international emergency assistance being given to Afghanistan. These assistance packages come from a wide range of donor countries and are primarily intended for direct support, clothing support and poverty alleviation. A significant share of such specified project assistance is the US$400 million aid package offered by the United States for relief and reconstruction. Thus USAID is playing a leading role in meeting the urgent need in Afghanistan for food, water, shelter and medicine. A series of programmes have been identified by USAID and this proposal has positioned these programme objectives within the Freedom Framework.

USAID project assistance

Strengthening democracy *(political freedoms)*
This seeks to build upon and increase existing Afghan capacities, both in the non-governmental and governmental sectors to reinforce democracy and stability.

Rebuilding infrastructure *(economic and social opportunities)*
The infrastructure that has been destroyed in the war is severely overburdened by returnees whose houses have been reduced to rubble and this project helps rebuild the urban infrastructure.

Rehabilitation of agriculture *(protective security)*
The country's food production capacity has been devastated and its farmers have been impoverished. Since agriculture is traditionally the largest and most important sector of the economy, USAID has pledged long-term support for its revival.

Empowering women *(political freedoms)*
In the post-Taliban situation, there is an urgent need to support the condition of women who need jobs, education and a social and political role in the future Afghanistan.

Improving health *(social opportunities)*
Under-served communities have been identified for access to basic services

and health education. There is special emphasis on maternal and child health, hygiene, water and sanitation, immunization and control of infectious diseases.

Restoring media *(transparency guarantees)*
This consists of rebuilding communications and journalistic capacity with the goal of informing and uniting Afghan people to help produce a peaceful, stable and viable political transition and administration.

Enhancing education *(social opportunities)*
There is a need to provide initiatives amongst teachers and children to return to school and other educational establishments.

Creating jobs *(economic security)*
Job creation is a vital component of economic revival and is fundamental to recovery.

UNDP project assistance
UNDP also provides vital assistance to the Afghan government with a two-pronged development strategy covering recovery and reconstruction and capacity development of the government.

The priorities for this strategy have been derived from a Preliminary Needs Assessment, which outlines the financial requirements of the recovery and reconstruction of Afghanistan. This assessment was presented to the Tokyo Conference in January 2002, which was attended by the World Bank, the Asian development Bank and the Islamic Development bank. This conference led to the formation of the Immediate and Transitional Assistance Programme (ITAP) in Kabul and Geneva in February 2002. ITAP identified the urgent activities that required help and was guided by the principles laid down by the Preliminary Needs Assistance programme.

Recovery and reconstruction
Following the formation of the Afghan Interim Government (formerly the Afghan Interim Authority, AIA), the UNDP assisted in formulating the Draft National Development Framework of the AIA through the Afghanistan Assistance Co-ordinating Authority (AACA). UNDP is supporting the AACA to take the lead in the tracking and analysis of aid flows. The central focus of UNDP is to build national capacity through a variety of programmes within the ACAA, the Ministry of Finance and several line ministries. It is providing the interim administration with a database and project approval package, which is tailored to Afghan needs to ensure effective access to aid data within the administration and for the UN, donor and NGO community.

The specific needs of the sectors requiring immediate help were evaluated in a series of Sector Needs Assessment Missions whose findings were combined to formulate the Joint Afghanistan Reconstruction Trust Fund (ARTF) whose contributors include the World Bank, the ADB and the Islamic Development Bank. This fund facilitates the Recovery and Reconstruction Strategy, which has the following components:

- Implementation of the Recovery and Employment Afghanistan Programme (REAP), aimed at the rehabilitation of Kabul's public infrastructure, creating in the process ready opportunities for employment. *(economic security)*

- Support of US $50,000 for logistics, coordination and needs assessments following the recent series of earthquakes. *(protective security)*

- Restoration of 30 offices for government ministers and other office buildings, including the barracks located next to the Office of the Chairman, and provision of office supplies and equipment for 30 ministers. *(political freedoms)*

- Rehabilitation of the Prime Minister's Palace including the premises of the AACA, assisted by Crown Agents, thus enabling the AIA to host the first Implementation Group meeting. *(political freedoms)*

- Leading a needs assessment mission on redevelopment and reintegration of the ex-combatants which resulted in recommendations for a major programme on which UNDP is expected to take the lead. *(social guarantees)*

- Development of a rehabilitation programme for local government offices in the provinces which is estimated at US$25 million and which is currently under discussion. *(political freedoms)*

- Designing of a national area-based programme, focusing on urgent rehabilitation of the socio-economic infrastructure to quickly reduce levels of poverty and hardship, and to allow for the return of people displaced through drought, war and economic hardship. The programme, tentatively estimated at US$60 million over the next five years, will target the following priority areas: Shamali Plains; Dari-Suf, Yak-aw-lang and Central Bamyan; Khawajaghar-Hazarbagh; Takhar-Badakhshan; Mazar Region; Heart-Ghor; Kandahar; Paktia-Paktika; and Eastern Nangharhar. *(social security and protective security and economic securities)*

- Organization of a conference on south-south cooperation in partnership with the Government of India, in order to facilitate the development of a credible, coordinated and transparent mechanism by which southern capacities and supplies can be easily and cost effectively channelled to Afghanistan. *(transparency guarantees)*

REAP is of specific importance to our concerns and has started assisting the AIA, principally the Municipality of Kabul and the Afghanistan Ministry of Public Works, in their efforts to repair the district's ravaged public infrastructure. The project has already given work to more than 9,600 Afghans for rehabilitation projects that are underway in 40 sites around Kabul. It is expected that the number of people employed will double rapidly and continue to grow. REAP intends to provide employment to an additional 18 000 unskilled Afghans on small scale public works and labour-intensive projects, such as rehabilitation of schools and health centres, road repairs, dredging of riverbeds and solid waste management. Drawing on the lessons learned during this initial phase and with the Project Implementation Unit now solidly in place, an extension of this initiative to 8 other cities, with a three-year budget of US$90 million and a target of 100 000 US$2/day jobs, is now under way. This two-pronged strategy of generating employment while restoring key infrastructure in Kabul contributes to a swift transition to peace, stability and development.

One of the projects is the rehabilitation of Kabul River, funded by a US$3 million grant from the Government of Japan.

Capacity building

The UNDP is assisting in developing the capacity of the government to deliver basic services to its people. In order to aggregate all donor contributions within the overall REMDP, the following services which will be delivered by UNDP have been codified within Sen's Five Freedom Framework.

- Timely operationalization of the Afghan Interim Authority Fund (AIAF) before the official inauguration of the AIA. UNDP mobilized US$65.8 million to cover immediate recurrent costs and ensure effective functioning of the AIA. Regular AIAF updates are provided on implementation. *(political freedom)*

- Supporting key commissions outlined in the Bonn Agreement, including the provision of logistical and office support for the Loya Jirga and Civil Service Commissions and their secretariats as well as provision of four national consultants for the setting up of the Civil Service Commission. Additionally, a consultant was provided to assist in the setting up of the Judicial Commission who organized a series of consultations and workshops with key actors in the justice sector, including the Supreme Court and the Minister of Justice. UNDP, in collaboration with the administration, has also sponsored a series of workshops with women judges, the faculty of Kabul university and Afghan lawyers and prosecutors. *(political freedom)*

- Assisting the AACA with the formulation of the draft national development framework and the systematic collection of data on ongoing and planned reconstruction projects by the international community; preparation of the implementation group meeting, including logistical support, transportation and accommodation to donor participants; as well as conference documentation services; *(transparency guarantees)*

- Setting-up of a satellite system to deliver internet connectivity and to establish the administrative arrangements for the Office of the Chairman. UNDP has procured a second satellite system to meet the AACA's urgent needs for internet connectivity. In partnership with the World Bank, UNDP is establishing an inter-ministerial intranet. In collaboration with the private sector, UNDP is organising basic IT training for AIA staff. *(transparency guarantees)*

- UNDP is strengthening the Office of Disaster Preparedness within the Office of the Chairman. *(protective security)*

- Mobilizing technical experts from the Afghan Diaspora through the TOKTEN Programme (Transfer of Knowledge Through Expatriate Nationals) to enhance national capacity in the AACA and the Ministries of Urban Development and Health. In order to identify Afghans ready to contribute skills to the reconstruction and development effort, UNDP has developed a first roster of over 1000 candidates for those interested in drawing upon the services of expatriate Afghans. *(social opportunities)*

- Economic recovery can only be achieved by restoring the freedom of movement and competition among others urban markets. The Kabul–Kandhahar–Herat Road is one of the most significant projects that will enable movement of goods, services and people across the country. The USA has committed US$80 million towards this project, supported by US$50 million from Japan and US$50 million from Saudi Arabia. The Asian development bank has estimated that a total of US$650 million will be needed over the next two and a half years in order to repair this road and other major thoroughfares comprising about 1770 kilometres of the country's 21,082 kilometres of roadway. *(economic facilities)*

Identifying the problem and designing the project

This contextual analysis provides the development history of obstructions and aspirations and the international assistance being provided to the Afghan government. The challenge is to aggregate all of the development activities into the proposed Freedom Approach programme. This is not a master plan with a checklist of activities leading to a successful urban recovery programme for Afghanistan. On the contrary the long-term goal is a master plan that formulates a process of ever-expanding freedoms for the people.

Development is enabled through the process of recognizing the citizen as the agent of change. Their constraints have to be addressed to enable them to realize their full potential to live the life they value leading and in the process contribute to the formulation of the urban recovery process for the nation.

Development through the master plan

The problems and potential solutions to the long-term development of Kabul city through its master plan can be seen from two aspects. On one hand, there are aspects that relate to generic issues that transcend the specificity of Kabul and are concerned with the general problems of war-damaged economies and cities. On the other hand, there are issues that relate directly to and are unique to Kabul. The Removing Unfreedom Urban Recovery Programme (REMDP) has been formulated in order to define these urban development goals and to ensure that they are shared with the national administration. It has three concerns which are arranged in hierarchical relationship and are explained as follows.

- The longer term Vision for Development, which is shared with the Afghan Administration.

- Implemented Projects directed by the master plan project offices in each target city with city level and national partners within the programme's framework.

* Community-based sub-projects executed through a number of district level site offices in each city at street level within the parameters of the projects defined in the programme and under the direction of each master plan project office.

The shared vision

The immediate question before us is how one can enable the citizens of each of the cities to expand their lives and livelihoods through measures that they value. These measures need to remove the obstructions that conflict with community value systems or physical coercions that form part of some higher ideal that is remote and not shared by the community. As we have explained earlier, cultural, tribal and religious conflicts can devastate development initiatives. Participation processes are promising as they exist primarily to remove cultural coercions through the discussion of differences with individuals at community level and the expansion of tolerance and respect. The resulting process reveals the hidden strengths and potentials of the nation.

Undoubtedly the broader goals of development form part of the larger ongoing international project of ever-increasing human freedom in all societies. This may seem to be a highly abstracted notion; but it is never the less possible to convert this abstract quest into an implementable strategy. Such a strategy provides a vision for future Afghan cities. It is not a vision of nineteenth century ideals of rigid physical formations of open spaces, boulevards, parks and institutions that are termed modern but remain remote from the lives of urban Afghan citizens. On the contrary, this proposal describes a vision for Afghan cities that can be put in place through the formulation of master plans that focus on human development goals.

In evaluating the modes and degrees of development that could be made available to the citizens of Kabul, one needs to identify the instruments that will provide the deeper development and distinguish these from resources that are seen simply as enablers of implementation. The instruments of development are the principal means of accessing rights and opportunities that help individuals to expand their potentials and capabilities.

In short, the vision of the master plan of Kabul is the realization of instruments that will enable the citizens to expand their opportunities.

Five interdependent instruments constitute this vision and have been described in greater detail earlier in this book. However we will repeat them here in light of the macro, national obstructions identified in the project context of Afghanistan.

Economic facilities

We need to identify how citizens can use the economic resources of the city, its hinterland and other territories for the purposes of consumption, production and trade and exchange. Access to these facilities includes the availability to finance potential opportunities and adequate space to carry on with earning or exploring new ways to earn livelihoods and endorse self-help solutions.

Social opportunities

These are the arrangements and choices of opportunities that the administration makes for education, healthcare and other essential community facilities that citizens require to expand their social and economic lives.

Protective security

The city administration needs to undertake measures to provide the necessary access for the protection of a social security net that prevents the consequences of poverty and suffering from increasing as the migrant population increases.

Transparency guarantees

Citizens need to be provided with guarantees of openness, necessary disclosures and rights to information and tangible evidence of trust so that the clauses of the social contract between the city administration and the citizens are always clearly defined and enacted.

Political freedoms

The opportunities that the citizens will have to determine who should regulate their local affairs and on what principles. Enshrined in this opportunity is the citizens right to evaluate authorities, to free expression and participation in the political process.

The master plan of the city will need to include a series of measures that will provide the static improved and codified infrastructure as well as the kinetic ever-changing flows that enable physical spaces and economic opportunities to be taken in a continuity of dynamism that is inherently temporary and flexible.

Programme framework

The five instruments of development described above will need to be placed within a physical master plan and the accompanying legislation that is specific to Kabul and its future. Such a programme framework would include within its ambit many of the programmes being initiated by the government as well as those of bilateral agencies working in Kabul. Such a framework would enable a large degree of cooperation to take place between agencies, which may be working in diverse sectors to their own agendas. The windows of this framework could be regarded as the five openings into which specific development projects would need to be placed.

Sub-projects

The master plan will initially define and frame the project work divided into a number of sub-projects. Examples of such sub-project categories would be, for instance, infrastructure, land development, heritage protection, education, social health, commercial development, legislation, building byelaws, tenure, micro-credit, self-employment, training, transportation, recreation, park development, environment, water supply, electric supply, etc. Such sub-projects would be envisaged with specific budgets depending on their importance within the priorities of the vision.

A boy goes to collect water in Jade Marwan, the main street of Kabul, its buildings in ruins following years of shelling and war.

(Didier Lefevre/ Panos)

These are the street level activities and are divided into a series of sub-project contracts for implementation. Sub-contracts would relate to employment programmes, road repair, micro-credit banks, internet facilities, restoration of buildings, rehabilitation of existing damaged buildings, programmes for green field projects, production of local level information bulletins, mapping, data collection, etc.

Kabul Master Plan project

The first of the programme projects is the Kabul Master Plan project. Its broader goal of formulating a five-year master plan document will be implemented simultaneously in conjunction with shorter-term immediate sub-project activity. This immediate activity is divided into a number of street level sub-projects that form the nuts and bolts of the urban recovery process. Such a strategy will counter the growing dangers of disillusionment by adopting participatory high visibility outputs that have immediate impact.

The Kabul Master Plan project will address all five freedoms while also addressing, in the first place, the increasing urban problems caused by the returnee migration pressures. The lack of adequate housing and increasing unplanned growth has led to degraded environmental conditions in the city, and the virtual collapse of city-level services and infrastructure. To this is added the obstruction of political freedoms by the inaction of weak local government administration and controls and mushrooming, unregulated informal commercial activities. These activities have spread on to the riverbank and valuable heritage sites that need protection. The increasing unemployment, unstable prices and general decay in the standards of living of Afghan society have generated considerable international awareness of the need for crisis prevention. In order to relieve the city from these seemingly uncontrolled forces the freedom proposal aims to primarily remove obstructions to the lives of these middle city inhabitants through an implementation strategy of immediate short-term as well as longer-term sub-projects that simultaneously protect the heritage sites.

We discussed earlier the NSDF in Mumbai and their innovative and replicable implementation strategy through the women's saving group.

It is possible that a sub-project along these lines would create working sub-communities for self-governance of migrant dwellers in temporary settlements. The savings group addresses gender inequalities and social responsibility while establishing the capacity to carry out their own surveys, identifying households by their savings book. Over time households can then be listed for re-housing and moved to transit camps before being resettled in self-owned homes.

End objective

In spite of the hope emanating from the recent political evolution and the establishment of the AIA, there are dangers of disillusionment arising unless the required social security nets and facilities are put in place rapidly. The REMDP addresses this aspect particularly so that measures are taken quickly to ensure a peaceful city that aligns itself to economic growth and prosperity by providing a wider framework and a secure longer-term vision that can encourage all actors (including donors) to participate in a shared goal. The projects, as well as the sub-projects envisaged by the programme will enable donors to seek concrete outputs that are revisionable with future input from the participatory process of communities. Consequently the comprehensive programme will be multi-objective, in accordance with Sen's ideals, in addressing immediate economic reforms through job creation opportunities, while addressing flexible macro-institutional reforms through an ongoing, ever-expanding participatory formulation process. Therefore the end objective of the programme restores and strengthens the basic urban fabric of society. The implementation of immediate short-term physical infrastructure sub-projects will aim at a number of conditions such as restoring ruined streets, unsafe paving conditions, unkempt and encroached parks, broken street furniture, neglected and inadequate children's parks, abandoned or misused archaeological sites, ruined and badly damaged urban fabric, extensive garbage heaps and unclaimed war damaged vehicles and machines

Construction activities are doing relatively better than other sectors of the economy and are likely to expand as economic activity recovers. This dependable financial activity offers the opportunity to train young people in some basic skills in all areas of the construction and housing field. The goal is to combine these skills with those created in removing the social obstructions, thereby increasing citizenship and providing leadership, equality, flourishing local economies and dynamic cultural participation. The process of restoring pride in the city, its heritage sites and values will reinvest the potential of individuals and communities to create futures worth living.

Project design: planning and implementation

Implementation is a multi-objective and complex part of the project stage. We are expecting to initiate actions at macro-national, regional and community level as well as micro (individual) level. We will be addressing actions in all the five domains of unfreedoms and working towards removing obstruction for individuals that have macro, meso and micro causes.

Urban recovery programmes in countries in crisis must address both short and long term solutions. Therefore the REMDP for Afghanistan proposes solutions at two levels that will run concurrently and be implemented in the field through the mechanism of sub-projects as explained in the proposal. The short-term solutions are intended to avoid prescriptive large-scale solutions for the city as a whole. The long-term solutions are intended to define the future vision for the city through the Kabul Master Plan project document.

The Freedom Approach, as explained earlier, is not determined by one person, agency or institution. The design of the implementation process is very specific to community participation and the process of re-ordering values. However as Afghanistan has no history or mechanism for participatory process with the government, a holistic urban recovery vision will be implemented through the formulation of the master plan project. This vision will be realized through the administrative office of a newly established Kabul Master Plan Project Office (MPPO) within the strengthened municipality and the national administration.

The short-term quick relief initiatives will be divided into a number of small-scale high priority sub-projects that will have a visible impact. In adopting this strategy, the project avoids the kind of problems large-scale projects inevitably encounter when the need is to restore citizen confidence in the administration as soon as possible. Large urban scale problems involve the repair and restoration of city infrastructure such as heating, electrical supply, gas and water and sewerage. These large-scale problems require a different order of funding and implementation time and are not included as sub-projects to be implemented in any aspect of the current project. Significant inputs from other donor aid projects are addressing this aspect.

The programme goals are directed at the preparation of the master plans of Afghan cities and the Master Plan Project emerging out of that is primarily intended to create a master plan for Kabul City through capacity building and social integration. The large-scale infrastructure projects that are being planned and funded by other donors will get positioned into the overall master plan. The proposal seeks to integrate the various independent initiatives that are concerned with urban recovery into the master plan framework.

This proposal does not tackle the serious problem of restoration and conservation of all of the historical monuments. Instead, the project has initially identified only the Babar Garden and the Timur Shah monument for exemplary restoration as well as some smaller community level monuments.

Public awareness and participation

A central part of the project strategy is to create public awareness of urban issues, which affect the lives of the citizens. The project's public awareness

Hazara children in war-torn Afghanistan shortly after the Taliban took Kabul.

(Martin Adler/ Panos)

campaign will run concurrently and be part of the broader programme campaign undertaken by the urban recovery programme.

Over the past years, and particularly under the Taliban regime in Afghanistan, there has not been any effort made by the central authorities to involve the general public in the planning or execution of Afghanistan's urban renewal and preservation works. The coercive nature of the regime did not ensure any genuine citizens' involvement. Formulating activities are necessary to build up a process of genuine public awareness and a system of public participation, discussions and inclusion mechanisms leading to self-governance capabilities.

The REMDP will focus on transparency guarantees and devise ways to create public awareness with regard to the objectives and ongoing processes of the master plan projects through the print, televised and audio media. For this, the MPPO may engage a media consultant to formulate and spearhead the public awareness campaign, in coordination with the national steering committee and local district level in Kabul. A key responsibility of the project director will be to provide the necessary administrative mechanisms to interact with citizens who have been encouraged by the public awareness campaign. This is particularly important in project activities related to the participation of private property owners who's listed building's facades may be identified for repair or restoration in the project's strategy. This awareness will be achieved through public participatory discussions, regular press articles, radio programmes and serialized television documentaries.

The issue of guidelines for upgrading private property as well as new developments in the project areas will be the responsibility of the MPPO. The criteria for inclusion of private buildings as heritage assets must be discussed and approved by the steering committee.

Vocational training

The focus on economic facilities will direct emphasis on vocational training. The selected technical and administrative personnel will be required to undergo a period of vocational training during which they will be divided into groups and given separate training in each of the skills required for implementing the project sub-contracts. Gender issues, which are considered more deeply within the political freedoms objectives, will be identified from the onset. It will be the responsibility of the MPPO to allocate the required vocational training for each of the technical staff, professional and administrative interviewed by them.

Vocational training skills will be imparted to these groups at institutional level and through NGO efforts. The identification of suitable national or international institutions to implement these training courses will be done according to agreed criteria established by the international consultants. Incentives for the trainees attending the training courses will be an allowance they will receive to be decided by the MPPO. In relation to the selection procedures, the steering committee should approve the necessary information to confirm the candidate's suitability and request the trainees to choose representatives among themselves to report individual social concerns and successes on a weekly basis.

Sub-project: culture and heritage

In discussions with the AIA, ministers, the Mayor of Kabul and other administrators of Kabul, the proposal has identified distinct areas in Kabul where the pilot sub-projects will take place. Two selected monument areas within the city requiring heritage protection form a separate sub-project under the Historic Cities Programme work that is already under way. A brief description of other sub-project areas of Kabul that have been identified as crucial and demonstrative to the master plan implementation arrangement have been described below.

Sub-project: data collection

The master plan requires that a current database be established to enable the planners to understand the post-Taliban situation of the city. This data is concerned primarily with two aspects. First, there is a need to re-map the physical condition of the city and second there is a need to prepare up-to-date statistics on the inhabitants of the city. The rapid changes in the demographic profile of Kabul during the post-Taliban period have altered the ground reality of the city, its population and its social mix.

Maps of the city and infrastructure

An international surveying consultant will prepare base maps for the city. These will be prepared in an office specially designated for this task in Kabul. Municipal authorities will identify surveyors who will act as national counterparts to the surveyors and build up the municipal capacity to carry out the subsequent district level surveys required for the zonal maps of the entire city. The built fabric, city infrastructure and the definition of plots and their ownership will eventually get recorded in the zonal maps. These maps will form the basis of the data on which the master plan will be made. Collection of statistical data about the population, household size as well as other social data necessary for the future planning of Kabul will be commissioned as part of this sub-project.

By its nature this sub-project will have the highest potential for identifying individuals and communities, particularly within the migrant populations. A central part of this interaction will be the need for a cultural participation component in establishing community-led surveys. Through identifying representatives for ongoing community survey training and reporting, this participation sub-project will have short and long-term objectives laying the ground for ownership of the knowledge about their communities and initiating deeper regional and community local governance capabilities.

Sub-project: housing recovery

Kabul's complex condition requires special initiatives. Its longer-term status as a prosperous capital city has been superseded by an economy in urgent need of stability. The larger umbrella programme and the Kabul City Master Plan project will need to address not just longer-term development goals but also shorter-term stabilizing objectives. The sub-projects will need to be conceived as flexible projects that will transform the shorter-term stability goals into longer-term transitional and developmental goals for a capital city. For this reason exclusive emergency relief and 'fire fighting' projects are not being considered. Instead, the Freedom proposal will promote projects that are identified for longer-term objectives but can be 'kick started' as urgent stabilizing influences.

The housing sub-project targets low-income communities and single woman-headed families and aims to rebuild their housing through labour-based and community participation approaches. Also included in the project target are municipal buildings. The development objective of the sub-project is to enable houses to be re-built in the districts by using expanded employment opportunities. To achieve the development objectives in a sustainable way, the project intends to create capacity at different levels. Previous capacities have been utterly destroyed as a result of the catastrophic war. The resultant income generation will inevitably improve living conditions and promote a vital sense of optimism. In the process, communities that have been dispersed by the ravages of ethnic conflicts will once again be restored to their rooted social networks.

Outputs

The most significant output of the sub-project will be the establishment of a city level building centre that will lead the integrated approach to urban recovery. Tthe concept of this project manages to anticipate and address the five freedoms that are interconnected in the process of re-building at the macro international, national level and the micro individual level. This form of analysis is crucial in the implementation of a Freedom urban recovery programme as it takes some thing seemingly simple, like a stock yard for building materials, and facilitates a variety of development mechanisms in order to further expand development goals.

Stock yard for building materials

The building centre will consist of a fenced yard, covered space for training and administration and dedicated staff. It will have two functions:

- as a stocking yard for essential building materials

- providing training and know-how in building skills.

Protective security

An enormous number of houses have been destroyed or damaged in the 16 districts of Kabul. There are also a number of community buildings (schools etc.), which have been severely damaged. A large number of international agencies are engaged in planning and implementing emergency repairs to protect the inhabitants from the humanitarian crises that exist. In addition, significant self-help efforts are also becoming visible.

Economic facilities

The re-construction process and the speed with which it will need to be conducted by all the agencies concerned will inevitably lead to enormous distortions in the market mechanism and in the pricing of cement, wood, blocks, sand, gravel, plumbing materials, electrical materials as well as a number of finishing items such as glazing and tiles.

Transparency guarantees

While private initiatives may be able to circumvent these price distortions through arrangements and understandings of mutual community relationships, the efforts of the international community in procuring building materials may be severely affected by price distortions. Where there is such dependence on imported materials, it is common to find monopolized sources emerging, particularly if heavy demand on crucial materials is expected. The building centre could regularly stock basic building material in the yard, which will act as a buffer to the private sector in case the cost of material is becoming prohibitive. Such materials would be issued by the municipality or NGO's working in the field of housing recovery.

Social opportunities

The building centre will provide:

- training for trade skills necessary for building works

- assistance to small construction enterprises, supplies for entrepreneurs and transport enterprises through a SME programme

- Supervision and monitoring services for the urban recovery sub-projects.

The project will have a significant presence in Kabul. However, the geographical spread of the sub-project sites will be determined to ensure compactness and high visibility while addressing the most urgent needs. A 'needs assessment' survey will precede the selection of the site locations. The implementation strategy will follow a dual strategy to distinguish between major and minor works. Major works only will be taken up and will be based on paid labour, material supply, direct execution or contractual execution as well as monitoring and supervision.

Political freedoms

The effects of a transparent and protected building economy allow for a greater ability to avoid fiscal crisis. The process will provide all participants – including individuals, communities and cities – with a greater sense of citizenship and stability to build on their success while gaining the confidence to formulate ongoing need alterations as they surface from the construction process.

Other sub-projects

Other sub-projects that the REMDP will address include: district level development; real estate opportunities and controls; physical infrastructure; housing policy; municipal capacity building for planning; land ownership and registration; and open spaces and physical environment recovery.

Project design: monitoring, evaluating and impact assessment

In order to evaluate the development of the nation, city and society as a whole, it becomes necessary to view the urban recovery programme and master plan proposal at two levels. The first level addresses the long-term realization and achievement of a future vision for the city. This is implemented through the MMPO. The achievements take place within the strengthened municipality status.

The second level consists of the short-term quick relief initiatives divided into small-scale high priority sub-projects that focus more on local communities and individuals. The large urban scale problems involved with the repair and restoration of city infrastructure such as heating, electrical, supply, gas, water and sewage are of a different order of funding and implementation time and are already targeted by other donor aid projects. However, integrating and evaluating the submission results that donors have provided from their initiatives in to a common Freedom evaluation procedure promises to yield a very dynamic level of cooperation. The process will allow the formulation of a shared platform for the evaluation of successes and failures.

Within in the Removing Unfreedoms approach it becomes necessary to evaluate the freedom status of the individuals who compose the group under evaluation. In regarding these individuals as agents of change rather than patients of diagnoses, or recipients of benefits, one aims to measure the capability and potential and the obstructions to that potential. By grouping obstructions according to the five instruments of freedom, it is possible to evaluate the obstructions in terms of unfreedoms.

Throughout the 30-month implementation process two principal monitoring and evaluation consultants, familiar with the Freedoms Approach, will visit the project site periodically and report after each visit. During the last four months of the project life all the activities and components of the project will be evaluated by appointed national consultants and the results made known to the steering committee, the MPPO, the municipality and will passed on to inform donors and disseminate lessons learned. At this point the focus for the Kabul Master Plan project must be to evaluate and disseminate all the information required to facilitate the rapid replication of the successful sub-projects in other cities in Afghanistan, starting with the city of Herat.

Political freedoms

The importance of the Removing Unfreedoms development approach to monitoring and evaluating the urban recovery project could not be of more significance for Afghanistan. Shortly, the nation's population will experience their first free elections for more than two decades. It is seen to be a key component in attempts to build democracy in the country after years of war. Nonetheless elections due for September 2004 have already been postponed from June 2004 and face further delays as officials say more than 20 Afghan parties are at odds over what sort of elections to hold, when they should take place and whether presidential and parliamentary votes should be simultaneous.[23] The UN has continuing concerns over security for voters, candidates and officials and a slower voter turnout after a spate of election-related attacks by militants opposed to the US-backed authorities in Kabul. The Taliban has vowed to disrupt the polls. Separately, Spain has pledged to send more troops to Afghanistan to help provide security for the UN-backed elections. About 1,000 soldiers would be sent before the polls, in the plan approved by the cabinet to be presented to parliament.

Culture and ethnic diversity

Central to this whole issue of development, political freedoms, participation process and democracy is the role of culture and the representation of the ethnic diversity of Afghanistan. At a recent NGO conference convened by the Japanese government in Tokyo, 11 out of 29 Afghan representatives came from the same province with one ethnic group occupying 20 seats and several ethnic groups having no representation at all (BBC 2004.) In order to give Afghans the opportunity to influence the direction of their country's reconstruction and development and encourage peaceful and tolerant relationships, an ethnically and geographically diverse advisory group could be chosen who would ensure that funds are disbursed in a manner that represents the inclusive concerns and priorities of Afghans from different parts of the country. A representative advisory group to the UN would be a first-step in giving Afghans a consistent mechanism for input into the reconstruction of their country. Certainly the design of the REMDP goes several steps further in specifying a monitoring and evaluation framework as part of the formulation and implementation process of ever-expanding freedoms.

Non-determined policy

The foundation of the Removing Unfreedoms approach is Sen's social choice theory that directs economic development policies to focus on values and the diversity of particular values within the universal. Therefore communities with their diverse circumstances and cultures are given preference over universal structures.

The issue of shared ethical principles is considered in a different way. Sen argues that an approach to development that centres on people should start by understanding the variances within universal morals and ethics governing the lives of different human beings. Therefore common moral and ethical urban development policies cannot be predetermined. Knowledge of particular constraints on the inhabitants of a community is to be gained at an intimate participatory level rather than as broad objectives assumptions based on general knowledge.

At the universal level, this approach respects principles regarding citizens' obligations and duties as part of our normative ethical system. At the particular level it highlights the need for new indicators and standards to improve the human condition for individuals within communities. The emphasis is on evaluating particularities such as capabilities and potentials, to ensure that citizens are regarded not as spectators or patients but as both participative and independent agents of change. When evaluating the particular there is a need to take into account the varying subjective wishes of individuals whose capabilities may be constrained by factors not necessarily common to all people. While a community as a whole may share many such constraining factors, the freeing of these obstructions may not relieve individuals. These variables will emerge out of citizens' desire to remove constraints preventing them from leading the life that they wish to live.

New indicators

Earlier in the book we suggested new indicators would provide an informational base with relative weights given to the five types of unfreedom.

Data could supply a cross measure between relative degrees of individual unfreedoms or obstructions within a community, as well as a basis for comparing the relative degrees of freedoms enjoyed by individuals in other communities. One could look forward to new indices being brought out reflecting the degrees of freedom enjoyed by communities.

Development policy will need to balance the human achievement outcomes of a policy between the different types of achievements that the community may need to choose, since all freedoms may not be accessible or realizable simultaneously. Policy makers may consider that, in the given circumstances of a case, it may be impossible to guarantee ideal political freedoms (as currently in Afghanistan) and policies would need to be devised that would distinguish between the long-term national level achievement goals and the shorter-term localized ones. Shorter-term goals could distinguish between constraints to freedom that have local origins. Such an approach would regard the overarching obstructions to freedom as an aggregate of constraints at different levels. A different level of policy may be required for enabling the removal of constraints that need funda-mental political and social transformations. The matrix for evaluation would emerge out of public discussions so that the weights given to the indicators are understood and agreed to by the community being surveyed. Public support is a precondition for identifying criteria for evaluation.

End of project situation

At the end of the project, Kabul city will have a master plan that has been endorsed by the Government of Afghanistan and commits to a Removing Unfreedom approach as required for all development initiatives. The estab-lishment of a full time MPPO will activate the ongoing formulation, imple-mentation and monitoring of the master plan, which will likewise co-ordi-nate the contributions of international donors and agencies. The formula-tion process of the master plan will have, as it foundation, the simpler Removing Unfreedom framework through which donors could address concerns based on their special historic links to Afghanistan as well as their own metropolitan compulsions. Donors will enter the current development field through this common framework and submit the results of their initia-tives to a common evaluation procedure, thus formulating a shared plat-form for the evaluation of successes and failures.

The AIA will have identified issues relating to the realization of the master plan that will need legislation in the form of decrees, national laws, city level byelaws and longer term policies. A series of short-term inter-ventions will have been initiated that will contribute to recovering the original spirit of Kabul that was once a unique city in the region and a major tourist destination. These interventions will play an important and positive demonstrative role to the citizens of Afghanistan and spark further spontaneous municipal initiatives and an overall positive synergy in the populations of the cities. It is very likely to bring economic returns in the short and medium term by attracting new investments in to the urban structures of the selected areas.

Beneficiaries

Importantly the social capital mechanisms at the heart of the REMDP will provide an ever expanding formulation process that integrates, on every level, political freedoms, economic facilities, protective security and transparency guarantees.

The first beneficiaries of the project will primarily be young children, who make up over half the population of the city. They will experience the confidence and security of living in an improving urban environment with hope and improved facilities. At the same time, all the citizens of Kabul will benefit from the refurbishment of crucial urban areas of the city as well as from the sense of optimism that the project will expect to bring to the day-to-day life of the inhabitants. The citizens of Kabul will benefit from the regularization of markets, integrated local economies, encouragement for private investment in real estate, and the general establishment of global links of the Afghan economy.

Kabul Municipality will benefit from the capacity building components of the project. It will be able to administer its affairs within the long-term vision that the master plan has proposed for Kabul. The activities will focus on the formulation of a public awareness strategy that continually provides the public with information about the purpose and achievements of the project. The Kabul municipality will benefit from the higher revenues that urban recovery will enable it to collect. At the same time, the programme will benefit from the expertise and the administrative infrastructure created by the Afghan municipality to tackle the implementation of the master plan project and reinforce international confidence in the economic prospects of Afghanistan. The master plan will facilitate the municipality's ability to respond actively to donor inputs aimed at relieving the immediate economic hardships caused by the economic restructuring and the establishment of a new democratic government. The replication of this project in other Afghan cities will endorse the objectives of the urban recovery programme.

From national policy, to city municipalities, to the growing migrant populations of the middle city, the urban recovery programme will establish a process that will enable the people to establish their role and choose where they want to place themselves in the rural urban spectrum and thus lead the lives they value leading. The far-reaching objectives of urban

development will of course address economic recovery through physical interventions. However, the REMDP will go beyond the specification of creating more jobs by responding to an ever-expanding human development process where both individuals and communities rediscover their hidden potentials and citizenship.

A woman gazes out over her city, Kabul, scarred by years of war.

(Andrew Testa/ Panos)

-13-

Looking Ahead

If we view the twenty-first century with foreboding regarding our future, we may agree that significant oppositions are emerging that challenge the dominant ideology of current development goals. And this opposition is not supported by just a few. There are certainly issues of importance that have been neglected and therefore opposition is to be expected. We believe there is a need to review the deeper causes that relate to the unwillingness of millions of people to accept a permanent condition of underdevelopment. Such neglected circumstances foster authoritarianism and violent solutions in the grasping for quick remedies to an unacceptable life. Authoritarianism feeds on unfreedoms and the related condition of underdevelopment of those who are thus ruled. Unfreedoms are continuously increased by authoritarianism through conflicts to enhance control.

We must challenge the literature of development theories that had occupied centre stage of economic thinking during the cold war and that is irrelevant for several reasons. For one, the projected expectations from the new millennium economics have become uncertain. This uncertainty touches on the future of all three economic blocks. In the industrialized world consumerism and supremacy of the free market forces have eroded the benefits of a Keynesian welfare sate. The second world is littered with the debris of the institutions of the Soviet systems. Social opportunities that have been taken for granted for decades have all but disappeared, leaving the citizens waiting on the road. Then there is the third world – the underdeveloped world – a world where the very notion of a nation state has been replaced in so many parts by autocracy, authoritarianism and a large dept. The World Bank informs us that 'the poor' have increased from 1.8 billion to 2.2 billion in this period – excluding China.

From a global perspective we are in a situation in which every donor and every country is willing to pursue any and every approach and policy to improve their situation. Multiple goals and targets have become acceptable in what seems an ocean of development problems. In these circumstances either one accepts the contention of some experts who describe the contemporary times as static times, when the plateau of post-modern, post-development and post-historical conditions will now prevail forever, or one believes there is a need to meet this challenge with the optimism of a new approach, a new vision for development polices based on what Amartya Sen has proposed. His is a new perspective, with new definitions and a new analysis of this contemporary reality. According to Sen we must describe our development goals in such a way that they are placed within the context of a larger more universal human development aspiration. Such a universal aspiration could be expressed not in terms of produce, income, poverty or prosperity but in the deeper search for expanding degrees of freedom for our children and ourselves.

Underdevelopment would be seen as a condition of imposed unfreedoms and the degree of underdevelopment would no longer be primarily a questioning of poverty. A country's track record of high economic growth rates is no longer sufficient or even adequate to evaluate its level of development or success, as prosperity in an authoritarian regime is as intolerable as poverty in a democratic regime.

There are those who would argue that it is possible to dismiss Sen's approach as just another people-centred approach that donors are already aware of. They might argue that Sen's ideas have already been tried and tested by NGOs and institutions dedicated to micro-level empowerment projects. In almost every discussion in connection with Sen's Freedom Approach we have faced the question as to whether this is yet another universal prescription. Development literature is full of universal prescriptions about development goals. Even in the field, the more typical NGO comment is that they are tired of smart academics that come at regular intervals to visit them with new theories of development and new ways to evaluate their achievements. For them, participatory work with the community would become endangered if they were to keep realigning their objectives to fit into the changing frameworks of development. Perhaps it takes longer to implement a development objective than to hold a development theory steady.

Development frameworks cannot be protected from the turmoil of every day. Development is heuristic and subject to continuous redefinition because its knowledge base is continuously growing. It is in this context that we place the importance of Amartya Sen's work. Today we can talk about sustainable human development because the knowledge base of what spurs human progress has expanded enormously. Human development has multiple targets, multiple agencies and multiple agendas.

We must accept the diversity of activities as well as the diversity of concepts as being part of the fundamental definition of urban development

Januz Zeqiraj, his
sons Visar (left)
and Veton (right)
and daughter
Venera arrive back
at their village,
Studenica,
Kosovo, to find
their home has
been totally
destroyed.

(George
Georgiou/
Panos)

today. Initiatives will have different bits and pieces that tend to rattle around in the box of development literature.

Essentially what Sen is saying is that it is possible to have a common overarching goal of development which can contain all of the development approaches as long as we redescribe these components and link them together as essential parts of an organic whole. He would name this overarching developmental goal 'Enhancing Individual Freedoms'. In defining this goal, Sen is asking us to consider some different ways to think about human development, particularly in three ways.

First, development goals eventually need to target the individual human being. The individual human being is society's most important component and its ultimate agent of change. Each human being is unique and wants to live a unique life. It is his or her fundamental right to be free and live the life that he or she values. The process of development is one that removes obstructions and enables the citizen to move closer to the life that he or she values. These values can have cultural and spiritual qualities and relate more to the satisfaction of exploring one's own potential and character. Increasing freedom is linked to development and can be translated. Freedom can be expanded through its five components or instruments that influence the potential of the citizen. These are the instruments that citizens need to enable them to overcome their constraints. More important these are the instruments that inform us of the degrees of unfreedoms that are prevalent in a society and hence the degree of underdevelopment.

The thrust of development needs to reach deeper than the community, and deeper than the household. Each human being has the ability to gain free agency but is often prevented from doing so by obstructions or constraints on his or her social, political and economic opportunities. The engine of continuous development is each citizen. Successful development is that which enables that citizen to constantly search for higher opportunities and a life of higher personal value. This does not preclude the possibility that such a search could be undertaken through collective support but it does mean that any collective obstructions do not take the priority and have to be addressed together with individual obstructions.

Second, that development will succeed if the process that removes these obstructions is a multi-objective strategy. This multi-objective strategy can be understood better if they are categorized into sub-headings which Sen calls the five freedoms. As we have explained earlier, freedom will be expanded through the five instruments that citizens need to enable them to overcome any obstructions. These are the instruments that inform citizens and policy makers of the degrees of unfreedom and underdevelopment that are prevalent in a society.

The five types of freedoms that individuals need are access to political freedoms, economic facilities and social opportunities, and to expect transparency guarantees and protective security. All five are interconnected and equally important. They are like the five equally important sides of a box in which development is contained. The fuller the development levels in the box, the lower the levels of obstructions. The obstructions to the five

Mustat Robbli, an asylum seeker from Kosovo who arrived in Glasgow in 1999 now spends most of his time in his flat, Glasgow, Scotland.

(George Georgiou/ Panos)

Contrast between old hutong quarter earmarked for development and new high-rise buildings, Chongqing, China.

(Mark Henley/Panos)

freedoms are thus the filters through which one can evaluate the level of development of an individual, a household, a community, a city or a nation. Ideally, a Freedom Index could be devised for micro and macro-observations.

The third aspect emphasized by Sen relates to evaluations and new frameworks. In order to redefine the ends of development with these new definitions, new evaluation methods and data will need to be gathered, data that will begin to inform us about citizens' aspirations and not government perceptions. Such data needs to be collected through demo-cratic discussions that evaluate the citizen's choices which could enable them to lead the life that they choose to lead and value. Therefore we should ask how does one measure the status of this freedom and hence the degree of urban development, or how does one evaluate whether any

obstructions have been removed? There will exist a system of evaluation, coordination and shared policy frameworks. Removing obstructions in the life of citizens of a community requires not only an integrated approach but also the help of a variety of institutions and agencies that take it on board as a social commitment. Enhancing development is therefore not something you can pick at in an isolated way; it does need to be supported by a social commitment to make it successful.

Old buildings being demolished in the Pudong district, Shanghai with skyscrapers of the new financial centre rising behind.

(Mark Henley/ Panos)

We cannot move forward without a common policy framework that is shared between city administrations. It is our belief that this common framework could be based on the five freedoms defined by Amartya Sen and that cities alliances could formulate shared charters of local governance that incorporate the five instruments of freedom as the guiding principles .As part of this shared city-to-city project, there is a need to re-evaluate the existing urban environment with additional new indices so that one could measure degrees of freedom rather than relying exclusively on measuring degrees of poverty. Additional indices are needed and include a broader Human Freedom Index whose constituent parts are the five instrumental indices, each of which would provide measures for the degree of instrumental freedom experienced by urban citizens.

We therefore have an opportunity to introduce change. In the coming century, it is the city that is going to be the crucial instrument of change. If we accept that this change is to be for the better, then let us strengthen and widen our city-to-city cooperation and share the ethical,

Nairobi Central
Business District.

(Crispin Hughes/
Panos)

social, political and economic goals of expanding freedoms across the developed and underdeveloped divide. The setting up of such a global monitoring mechanism would enable the conclusions of shared evaluation indices to be integrated into common charters. This would be available to governments as well as donors as the basis for identifying policy goals and would enable them to make comparisons across cities. And once we agree to do that, we can re-evaluate the conditions of our cities with new indices that measure the causes and not the symptoms of underdevelopment.

With 528,000 residents, Kibera is the largest of Nairobi's 'informal settlements'. Its nine 'villages': are squeezed between the city centre and the wealthy suburbs of Karen, Lang'ata and Lavington, reserved in colonial times for European settlement.

(Crispin Hughes/ Panos)

Looking ahead the city of tomorrow will not be obsessed with physical formations alone but will be a city of multiple values. A city that needs to provide opportunities for a process of expanding real freedoms through its growth process. The design of the city will need to encompass both the static physical buildings and institutions, in the regulatory traditional sense of physical plans, as well as the kinetic spontaneous interactions of the inhabitants interchanging their perceptions, experiences, values and expressions. Both these components constitute the life of the middle city that effectively provides the entire macro-city with vibrant culture.

Kibera Slum.
Mashimoni
Squatters'
Primary School,
Nairobi.

(Crispin Hughes/
Panos)

The dynamism of the life of the city is released by the interaction between the static and the kinetic components of the middle city. It is this interaction that spurs the growth process in the city. As in all macro-urban cultures, the written rules tend to become rigid laws that need re-evaluating from time to time. They need to be framed not around the static ideal city configurations. On the contrary, the macro-city must be receptive to the ever-changing fluid situations that characterize the informal, undocumented, oral traditions of those whose identities are not, nor can ever be defined by an identity card.

The inhabitants of the middle city culture exist and they need to be accepted and their development as individual citizens encouraged. This is the other half of the city – the half that remains always as a temporary phenomenon and mediates its use of space and forms and occupies the cityscape where the byelaws must become more permissive not restricted. The life of the middle city creates a turbulence that results from this interchange and moves onward to an unpredictable destiny. It has the quality of a moving stream in which both tolerance and tensions are the energies that create new opportunities. The design and formation of our future city would therefore provide for the necessary processes and opportunities to develop for 'ever-expanding freedom'. This freedom is the end and means of the identity and character of the city of the future.

About the authors

Romi Khosla has for 25 years been the principal of a planning and architectural practice in Delhi. He graduated in Economics at the University of Cambridge, and in Architecture at the Architectural Association in the United Kingdom. His professional work includes the United Breweries Headquarters in Bangalore, the Semi-conductor Complex in Chandigarh, the Spastic School in New Delhi, the Meridian Hotel in Kathmandu and the National Gallery of Modern Art in Bombay. His regional planning work has been carried out for National and State Governments for the Kulu Valley in Himachal, the Lakshwadeep and Andaman islands, and Leh in Ladhak. His professional work has always encompassed concerns about economic development, architecture, urban planning and conservation. During the past six years, as a principal international consultant to the UNDP, UNESCO, UNOPS and WTO, he has spent considerable time initiating development projects linked to urban renewal in the Balkans, Palestine, Tibet, Central Asia, Cyprus and China. He is a senior consultant to INTACH and was a member of the Master Jury of the Aga Khan Award for Architecture. Khosla's writings have been extensively published in India and abroad; they include *Buddhist Monasteries in the Western Himalayas*, (Ratna Pustak Nepal 1979), *Future Schools in Palestine* (2000) and *The Loneliness of a Long Distant Future* (2002). Khosla originally studied economics with Amartya Sen. Over his years as an architect, planner and UN adviser, he began to appreciate that the solutions to the conflicts and poverty could be addressed through applying the economic considerations of Sen. He is the author of UN-HABITAT 'Removing Unfreedoms' discussion paper in 2002.*

Jane Samuels is architect consultant and visiting practitioner to the Centre for Development and Emergency Practice at the Oxford School of Architecture. She received a BA in Literature and Criminal Justice from the University of California, Berkeley and retrained at HRH The Prince of Wales's Foundation of Architecture and East London School of Architecture. She specializes in providing social, ecological and intercultural components with knowledge of participatory approaches. She has consulted on winning design team competitions for national and multi-national building projects. For 23 years she has taught residential and international workshops with a special interest in multi-cultural heritage of oral traditions. Jane was responsible for organizing the interview between Amartya Sen and Romi Khosla for the TVE film *Agents of Change* broadcast on BBC World television and at the World Habitat

Day presentation in Brussles and further meetings with Amartya Sen and the LSE colloquium. She authored and edited the research to the Mumbai workshops, the Removing Unfreedoms website and four volume report to the UK Department for International Development. Jane is responsible for preparing the material for publication in this book including edited transcripts, talks and reports. Previous articles, publications and talks include *World Architecture* magazine, *Building for a Future*, *Eco-Design*, UIA Congress Bursa 2003 collected papers, a UN-HABITAT Discussion Paper and CD-Rom compilation, 'Globalisation for the Common Good' conference, Dubai March 2004, and 'In Search of a Humanised Globalisation' conference, Japan April 2004.

Michael Mutter was, until recently, head of the Urban Development Group at DFID, where he spearheaded new approaches to multi-lateral development cooperation recognizing the direct input that community groups can make to policy making on an international scale and platform. He is now further developing financial mechanisms that bring development.opportunities more directly to the urban poor, working with UN-HABITAT and the broad group that make up the global Cities Alliance. From his position as the Urban Development Adviser at DFID, Mutter has been able to build a perspective of development encompassing new multilateral approaches as well as direct support to the entirely local initiatives of the UK NGO Homeless International, and SPARC, India, together with the growing Shack/Slum Dwellers International networks across the globe. In June 2002, at Trinity College, Cambridge, Mutter discussed with Romi Khosla and Professor Amartya Sen the importance of the Removing Unfreedoms concept to Urban Development as a key element in considering a developing world and reducing poverty in the twenty-first century.

> *"Global policy can bring development opportunity to an effective level of operation, integrating myriad players at differing levels, international, national and local, for differing inputs to development processes. The key is allowing development to take place without interference, bringing opportunity to the people who can take the lead responsibility. The international community can assist in developing such policies."*

Nesreen Berwari was recently awarded the UN-HABITAT Scroll of Honour in recognition of her extensive work in post-conflict reconstruction and resettlement of destroyed communities in the Kurdistan region of northern Iraq. Having initially served with the International Organization for Migration and UN relief agencies, she later directed a UN-HABITAT field office. Following completion of graduate studies in public policy and management at Harvard University's Kennedy School of Government, she served as Minister of Reconstruction and Development in the Kurdistan Regional Government that began the process of Removing Unfreedoms over a decade ago. Currently, Ms. Berwari has been serving at the national level as Minister of Municipalities and Public Works (MMPW) and most recently was reappointed to the Interim Government of Iraq that will administer the country from 1 July 2004. MMPW, with representation in over 300 municipal areas throughout the country, seeks to improve participation through representative sub-national governance.

> *"Service delivery can be improved by sound policy making at the national level and by reforming and reinvigorating the delivery of essential services through development of sub-national good governance at the provincial and municipal levels. Both global and national policy makers can learn from the Iraqi Kurdistan experience of devolving authority and responsibility to the village level where, given the freedom and the opportunity, development can be successfully led by the people themselves."*

Antonio Vigilante is the UNDP Resident Representative and UN Resident Coordinator for operational activities in Egypt. He is also currently the Chair of the Donor Assistance Group in Egypt. He was UN-Coordinator for Bulgaria responsible for commissioning Romi Khosla's Beautiful Bulgaria urban recovery programme now replicated in 106 cities in Bulgaria. Antonio was a key speaker at the July 7th Colloquium and presented crucial questions to Professor Amartya Sen and Lord Meghnad Desai. Antonio has taken an active interest in the Removing Unfreedoms project since it began and throughout the process provided constructive advice and support.

Alberto Lopes is an Architect, Urban Planner and Master in Organisation and Management of Territory, performing activities in urban development, urban planning, housing, and urban environment. He is member of the technical staff of the Brazilian Institute of Municipal Administration as researcher, professor and consultant all around Brazil. Member *ad honorem* of the Experts Regional Group for the Global Campaign for Secure Tenure of UN-Habitat/ROLAC. He worked in Ecuador as consultant of UN-Habitat, in Mozambique in a project sponsored by UNDP, and in Brazil with the Development Planning Unit (DPU) of University College, London. He attended the Removing Unfreedoms Colloquium at the London School of Economics. He has an award in Urban Planning bestowed by the Institute of Brazilian Architects and was born in Rio de Janeiro, Brazil.

Acronyms and Abbreviations

AACA	Afghanistan Assistance Co-ordinating Authority
AIA	Afghan Interim Government
AIAF	Afghan Interim Authority Fund
ARTF	Afghanistan Reconstruction Trust Fund
CENDEP	Centre for Development and Emergency Practice
CLIFF	Community-led Infrastructure Finance Facility
CPM	Capability Poverty Measure
DESTIN	Development Studies Institute
DFID	Department for International Development (UK)
DPU	Development Planning Unit
GNH	Gross National Happiness (Bhutan)
GNP	Gross National Product
HDI	Human Development Index
HDR	Human Development Report (UNDP)
IBAM	Brazilian Institute of Municipal Administration
IDCA	International Development Cooperation Agency
IEA	Interfaith Encounter Association (Israel)
IIED	International Institute of Environment and Development
ITAP	Immediate and Transitional Assistance Programme
LSE	London School of Economics
Mande	Monitoring and Evaluation News
MDG	Millennium Development Goal(s)
MPPO	Master Plan Project Office (Kabul)
NDSF	National Slum Dwellers Federation (Mumbai)
OECD	Organisation of Economic Cooperation and Development
PNA	Palestinian National Authority
PRAMS	Participatory Rights Assessment Methodologies
REAP	Recovery and Employment Afghanistan Programme
REMDP	Removing Unfreedoms Urban Recovery Programme
SDI	Slum (or Shack) Dwellers International
SLUMS	Strategic Low-income Urban Management Systems
SPARC	Society for Area Resource Centres
TBA	Traditional Birth Attendant
UNDP	United Nations Development Programme

Participating Organizations

Centre for Emergency and Development Practice (CENDEP)
Oxford School of Architecture
Oxford Brookes University
Gipsy Lane Campus
Headington
Oxford OX3 0BP
United Kingdom
Fax: 01865 483298
E-mail: rgiddy@brookes.ac.uk

The Cities Alliance
Cities Without Slums
Mailstop H5 - 501
1818 H Street, NW
Washington DC 20433
United States
Tel: +1 202 473 9233
Fax: +1 202 522 3224
E-mail: info@citiesalliance.org
Website: www.citiesalliance.org

Development Planning Unit (DPU)
University College London
9 Endsleigh Gardens
London WC1H 0ED
United Kingdom
Tel: +44 20 7679 1111
Fax: +44 20 7679 1112
E-mail: dpu@ucl.ac.uk
Website: www.ucl.ac.uk/dpu

United Kingdom Department For International Development (DFID)
1 Palace Street
London SW1E 5HE
United Kingdom
Tel: 0845 300 4100 (local call rate from within the UK)
Tel: +44 1355 84 3132
Fax: +44 1355 84 3632
E-mail: enquiry@dfid.gov.uk

International Institute for Environment and Development (IIED)
3 Endsleigh Street
London WC1H 0DD
United Kingdom
Tel: +44 (0) 20 7388-2117
Fax: +44 (0)20 7388-2826
E-mail: info@iied.org
Website: www.iied.org

Interfaith Encounter Association (IEA)
Dedicated to promoting peace in the Middle East through participatory interfaith dialogue and cross-cultural study.
Office: Ha'arazim Street, entrance 28 17 Jerusalem 96348, Israel
Address: P.O. Box 3814, Jerusalem 91037, Israel
Tel: + 02 6510520
Fax: + 02 6510557
E-mail: office@interfaith-encounter.org

Homeless International
Queens House
16 Queens Road
Coventry CV1 3DF
United Kingdom
Tel: +44 (0) 24 76632802
Fax: +44 (0) 24 76632911
E-mail: info@homeless-international.org
Website: www.sparc.org

London School of Economics (LSE)
Development Studies Institute
London School of Economics and Political Science
Houghton Street
London WC2A 2AE
United Kingdom
Tel: +44 (020) 7955-7425
Fax: +44 (020) 7955-6844

Mande NEWS
A news service focusing on developments in monitoring and evaluation methods relevant to development projects and programmes with social development objectives
Monitoring and Evaluation News
Edited by Rick Davies
Cambridge
United Kingdom
E-mail: editor@mande.co.uk
Website: www.mande.co.uk

Removing Unfreedoms
Citizens as Agents of Change in Urban Development
United Kingdom
E-mail: contact@removingunfreedoms.org
Website: www.removingunfreedoms.org

Slum Dwellers International (SDI)
P.O. Box 14038
Mowbray 7705
Cape Town
South Africa
Tel: +27 21 689 3748
Fax: +27 21 689 3912
E-mail: sdi@courc.co.za

Society for Promotion of Area Resource Centres (SPARC)
Mumbai
India
E-mail: admin@sparcindia.org
Website: www.sparcindia.org

United Nations Development Programme (UNDP)
One United Nations Plaza
New York NY 10017
United States
Tel: +1 212 906 5558
Website: www.undp.org

UN-Habitat
Information Services Section
Office of the Executive Director
UN-HABITAT
P.O. Box 30030
Nairobi
Kenya
Tel: +254 20 623120
Fax: +254 20 623477
E-mail: infohabitat@unhabitat.org

World Bank
Headquarters
Urban Development
The World Bank
1818 H Street N.W.
Washington DC 20433
United States
Tel: +1 202 473-1000
Fax: +1 202 477-6391
E-mail: urbanhelp@worldbank.org
WEbsite: www.worldbank.org

WSP Group PLC
First Point
Buckingham Gate
Gatwick Airport
West Sussex RH6 0NT
United Kingdom
Tel: +44 (0)1293 602 600
Fax: +44 (0)1293 602 699

Notes

1. See also the specific Millennium Development Goal, within the Sustainable Development Goal section, the Target of a significant improvement in the lives of at least 100 million slum dwellers by 2020.

2. See Mutter in Jones and Nelson (2002).

3. CLIFF is funded through the Cities Alliance with initial grants from DFID and SIDA.

4. See *Bridging the Finance Gap*, Homeless International 1999, research funded by the DFID EngKaRs programme.

5. C3 – the City-Community Challenge Fund pilots are being undertaken by the Joint UN Urban Management Programme involving UN-HABITAT, UNDP, and the governments of Netherlands, Sweden, Switzerland and UK.

6. 'Localising the Habitat Agenda for Poverty Reduction' is a joint research programme between UN-HABITAT and the Max Lock Centre at the University of Westminster, London, UK, funded by DFID.

7. The discussion documents an interview at Cambridge in September 2002, filmed by TVE as *Agents of Change*.

8. Interview discussion: 7 July Colloquium 2003, London School of Economics.

9. Max Lock Centre and WEDC 2002.

10. The discussion documents an interview at Cambridge in September 2002, filmed by TVE as *Agents of Change*.

11. Interview discussion: 7 July Colloquium 2003, London School of Economics.

12. A quotation attributed to Hazreti Ali. Muhyiddin Ibn Arabi, Kernal of the Kernal Beshara Publications, 1981.

13. Emerson, Caryl (1997), *The First Hundred Years of Mikhail Bakhtin*, Princeton University Press, New Jersey, USA.

14. Translated by Vincent A. Smith in *Ashoka*, S. Chand, Delhi, 1964, pp. 170-171 and quoted in Sen (1999).

15. We mean the long-term governmental policies installed to shift and improve the lives of the poor population living in the favelas out of physical and infrastructural intervention, without providing sound investments for the promotion of their citizenship and their social and educational improvement.

16. His Holiness the Dalai Lama of Tibet, Glasgow Convention Centre, June 2004.

17. A Pilgrimage to the Source of Interfaith and International Development Objectives.

18. Arjun Appadurai, 'The Capacity to Aspire: Culture and the Terms of Recognition', *Culture And Public Action* Edited by Vijayandra Rao and Micheal Walton, World Bank/Stanford University Press, California, 2004.

19. Interview discussion: 7 July Colloquium 2003, London School of Economics.

20. Lord Meghnad Desai, speaking at the 7 July Colloquium 2003, London School of Economics.

21. These conversations form part of an interview between Sheela Patel and Romi Khosla in Mumbai in May 2003.

22. The chapter draws on a report originally written by Romi Khosla for the Aga Khan Trust for Culture, April 2003.

23. *Refugees International*, June 2004.

References

Ardalan, N. (1973) *The Sense of Unity, The Sufi Tradition in Persian Architecture*, University of Chicago Press and London.

BBC (2004) South Asian News Online 'Afghan vote faces further delay' 4 July.

Choay, F. (1969) *The Modern City: Planning in the 19th Century*, G. Braziller, New York.

Cruikshank, J. (1992) 'Oral tradition and material culture', *Anthropology Today*, 8 (3), June.

DFID (2001) *Meeting the Challenge of Poverty in Urban Areas*, DFID, London.

DFID (2002) *Communicating Good and Best Practice in Different Cultural Contexts*, Annex L, March

DFID (2003) *Removing Unfreedoms*, DFID Report, Vol. 4, November.

Dreze, J. and A Sen (2002) *India, Development and Participation*, Oxford University Press, New Delhi.

Economist, The (2002) 'The Brown Revolution', *The Economist*, London, 9 May.

Emerson, Caryl (1997), *The First Hundred Years of Mikhail Bakhtin*, Princeton University Press, Princeton, New Jersey

Hobsbawm, E. (2000) *The New Century: in conversation with Antonio Polito*, translated from the Italian by Allan Cameron, Little Brown, London.

Howard, E. (1902 reprinted 1946) *Garden Cities of Tomorrow*, Faber and Faber, London.

Jones, S. and N. Nelson (Eds) (2004) *Practitioners and Poverty Alleviation*, ITDG Publishing, London.

Khosla, R. (2000) *Future Schools in Palestine*, UNESCO, Paris.

Lloyd-Jones, A. and C. Rakodi (Eds) (2002) *Urban Livelihoods*, Earthscan, London.

Lopes, A. (2004) *To Improve the Favela or to Promote Their Inhabitants' Status*, BIMA, Rio.

Max Lock Centre and WEDC (2002), *Localizing the Habitat Agenda for Urban Poverty Reduction*, London

Mumford, L. (1961) *City in History: Its Origins, Its Transformations and Its Prospects*, Harcourt, Brace and World, New York.

Mutter, M. (2001) *The Inclusive City: The Challenge of Urban Poverty Policies and Practice*, DFID Working Paper, DFID, London.

Naser, S. (1999) *The Spiritual and Religious Dimension of the Ecological Crisis*, Temenos Academy, The Prince of Wales's of Architecture, England.

Oliver, P. (1977) *Encyclopedia of Vernacular Architecture*, Cambridge University Press, Cambridge.

Payne, G. (Ed) (2002) *Land Rights and Innovation*, ITDG Publishing, London.

Patnaik, P. (2002) 'Introduction' in Sen, A. *The Loneliness of the Long Distant Future*, Tulika Books, New Delhi.

Perlman, J.E. (2002) *The Metamorphosis of Marginality*, Trinity College, February.

Ramesh, R. (2004) 'Another rewrite for India's history books, *The Guardian*, 26 June.

Redfield, R. and M.B. Singer (1954) 'The Cultural Role of Cities', *Economic Development and Change* 3: 53-73.

Rostow, W.W. (1960) *The Stages of Economic Growth: A Non-Communist Manifesto*, Cambridge University Press, Cambridge.

Satterthwaite, D. and A. Jonsson (2001) *The Limitations of Income-based Poverty Lines*, IIED Working Paper, IIED, London.

Sen, A. (1999) *Development as Freedom*, Oxford University Press, Oxford

Sen, A. (1970) *Collective Choice and Social Welfare*, Holden-Day, San Francisco

Sen, A. (1968) *Choice of Techniques*, 3rd ed. New York: A. Kelley.

Soros, G. (2002) *On Globalization*, Public Affairs Ltd, Oxford.

Stewart, F. (2002) *Horizontal Inequalities: A Neglected Dimension of Development*, WIDER Annual Lectures, WIDER, Helsinki.

Stites, R. (1989) *Revolutionary Dreams: Utopian Vision and Experimental Life in the Russian Revolution*, Oxford University Press, New York.

Turgut, H. (1990) 'Homelessness in Turkey as a result of the squatter phenomenon', *Open House International*, 15 (2&3).

UNDP (1996, 2000) *Human Development Reports*, Oxford University Press, New York.

UNESCO (1998) *A Cultural Approach to HIV/AIDS Prevention and Cure*,Website

UN-HABITAT (1996) *The Habitat Agenda*, UNCHS Habitat. Nairobi .

Index